"*What struck me the most about this book was the detail for which the author goes. She digs so deeply into her experience that it can be shocking, even to someone like myself, who has been through a similar experience. The writing is honest, courageous, and full of the emotion she has carried with her over the years.... The end of the book includes an essay by the author's husband who has been by her side for the last few years and was involved in her recovery. It's a poignant account of the struggle that he went through in trying to help his wife learn to be herself. This is a heart-wrenching and unique story that goes deep inside the mind of a bulimic.*"

—Lori Henry—Author of *Silent Screams*

"*I want to thank Jocelyn for her courage to write this brutally honest book about her long battle with bulimia and the courage to take on the challenge of informing the world and saving others. Her story has deeply touched me and reminds me in many ways of my own battles with bulimia. I strongly recommend this book to both young and older women.*"

—Andrea Roe—Author of *You Are Not Alone—The Book of Companionship For Women Struggling With Eating Disorders*

LEARNING

TO BE ME

LEARNING

TO BE ME

My Twenty-Three-Year
Battle with Bulimia

Jocelyn Golden

iUniverse Star
New York Lincoln Shanghai

LEARNING TO BE ME
My Twenty-Three-Year Battle with Bulimia

iUniverse Star
an iUniverse, Inc. imprint

iUniverse books may be ordered through booksellers or by contacting:

iUniverse
2021 Pine Lake Road, Suite 100
Lincoln, NE 68512
www.iuniverse.com
1-800-Authors (1-800-288-4677)

ISBN: 978-1-58348-482-1 (pbk)
ISBN: 978-0-595-87752-2 (ebk)

Printed in the United States of America

This book is dedicated to all those who have helped me on my journey of learning to be me.

Those who through random acts of kindness over the years gave me more comfort than they could ever have known.

My anonymous friends who have found me through my Web site; your struggles, stories, and words of encouragement inspire me.

Above all this book is dedicated to some very special, magical people who I will carry forever in my heart: Shosanna, Avis, Barbara and Elaine, wonderfully insightful therapists and warm, caring, giving people; Dr. Kanofsky who delivered my most precious son and helped me through a bulimic pregnancy with such compassion.

To my husband who believed in me even when I didn't believe in myself. I love you.

Finally to Jake, my beloved son and most precious gift in life.

Contents

Prologue

What follows is the true story of my twenty-three-year battle with bulimia. From its innocuous beginnings when I was thirteen, it took me on a journey of violent self-abuse that brought me to the edge of complete self-destruction. It left me so physically damaged that I required two life-altering surgeries and, as a result, I am reminded every day of the road I have traveled. Along the way my cries for help went unheard or were misunderstood and my utter reliance on and immersion in my disease eclipsed and overshadowed everything else. It was not until nearly a quarter of a century of living every aspect of my life through this disease that I found the strength, inspiration, and support to seek the help that finally brought me into recovery and enabled me to live without my most enduring companion, bulimia.

Today I am sharing this story with you, whoever you are—sufferer, friend, family member, spouse—in the hope you can spare yourself or someone you love from taking a journey similar to mine. If I can give you or your loved one the gift of self-kindness and resisting the false promises bulimia or other eating disorders offer, then my journey will not have been in vain.

PART I
THE PROMISE

Chapter 1

The Devil in the Bushes

I woke to the annoying buzz of my alarm, took a quick shower, dressed, and headed straight to the kitchen. Breakfast was my favorite meal because I loved cereal and I looked forward to it everyday. If I'd had my way, I'd have eaten cereal all day long and not much else. I never tired of consuming mouthfuls of crunchy Fruit Loops or chocolaty Cookie Crisps. I could eat bowl after bowl, and often would combine cereals to feel as though I was getting the best of both worlds. Along with my cereal, I simply had to have toast. I'd pop several slices of white Wonder bread into the toaster, and then spread a thick layer of butter and globs of jelly to melt all over the warm pieces. For a mouthwatering beverage, I'd poor myself a huge glass of thick, pulpy Sunny Delight orange juice.

Something was different this morning, though, after I devoured my breakfast. My stomach ached like no other ache I had ever experienced before, and I felt as if I was going to explode. I looked down to where the pain was concentrated and to my shock and dismay, I couldn't see my feet, not even the tip of my big toe. My protruding stomach was the only visible body part. *What am I doing? What am I thinking, eating bowl after bowl of sugary cereal and slice after slice of butter-dripping toast? I'm fat and eating like a pig. There's no way I can go to class feeling like this.*

I was supposed to meet my neighbor in ten minutes so we could walk to school together. Okay, Jocelyn, relax, take a deep breath, these feelings will go away, I reassured myself. I got my books and walked out the front door, hoping through some miracle the discomfort I felt would disappear, but it didn't.

I panicked. I simply had to do something right there and then. I couldn't stand it a second longer. I looked around—nothing. Then right in front of my eyes I saw my opportunity—the bushes. I hid under their cover and made myself throw up. I could taste the acidic vomit as I bent over in my hiding place with three fingers shoved as far down my throat as possible. One more attempt and all the food I'd just eaten sprayed onto the ground right in front of me. I could make out the Fruit Loops and the Cookie Crisp cereals I'd devoured only minutes ago. The toast and orange juice, too, splattered on the ground. There. Everything was out of me. I was completely empty.

I wasn't concerned with being caught. I didn't think of any potential harm to myself. I thought only of my discomfort and depression and how I couldn't face another day at school feeling as I had.

I was surprised to discover it took me only a few minutes to throw up all the breakfast I'd just eaten. I looked at the disgusting vomit on the ground. My cereal, toast, and orange juice stared right back at me. But instead of feeling disgusted with myself, I felt a peculiar sense of comfort. I didn't know this new feeling, which I thought might be a way to gain self-control and increase my self-worth, would turn to one of self-destruction.

With little time to spare before meeting my neighbor, I contemplated what I had done and realized I not only felt a sense of comfort but also something more. I no longer felt as if I would explode from being so full. I didn't feel as heavy or as fat as I did just minutes ago. As I walked up the road to meet Karen, I continued to process what had just happened as best I could. I discovered I wasn't ashamed of putting my fingers down my throat to make myself throw up. Rather, a new sensation pumped through my veins. I was calm. For the first time in as long I as I could remember, I went to school feeling that my lumps and bumps wouldn't grow as the day passed. I felt euphoric. A deep sense of serenity had followed the strange rush that throwing up provided. *This is crazy thinking,* I said to myself, but I had no more time to think about it. Karen walked out of her house, smiling and waving to me. I had to act normal, go to school. From that moment forward, the terrible, burdensome secret remained with me.

As the day progressed, I thought more about what had happened that morning. As I went from class to class, I couldn't focus on my subjects. I wondered if I would try throwing up again. Because the whole incident had happened so fast, all the conflicting feelings I had held in began to surface. I still felt relief, but I also started to think I had done something terribly wrong. Panic and guilt consumed me. I promised myself I wouldn't tell anyone about my eating and throwing up, even if for some reason I decided to do it again. I wasn't sure what it all meant. The day was a haze of confusion. I was plagued with the question, "How can food give me pleasure, relief, and shame all at the same time?"

In the ensuing days, I ate my usual favorite foods, cereal and toast, and again I made myself throw up. I didn't wait long—I did so that very same week. I decided, though, instead of going outside to hide in the bushes, I would slip into the bathroom to throw up all the food I'd just consumed. The binging and purging that first week turned into the next week and the next into the next. Little by little, I started to eat and throw up more and more. I decided not to limit throwing up to mornings. Anything I ate after school I figured I should get rid of as well. This way I could still eat but not fear all the things I associated with food: being even fatter, unworthy, unloved, and unliked. Within two months I was addicted to what I now considered to be very shameful behavior.

Because I was now binging and purging several times a week, I'd carefully observe others while they were eating. I felt like a food spy. Every lunch hour as my friends and I sat at the long wooden table in the gymnasium, I would look to see what they were having for lunch and how much they ate. Not once did I notice any of them looking as if they felt guilty about what they were consuming. They seemed to notice little about what they put in their mouths and were more concerned with laughing and socializing with one another. Then, during homeroom, I'd sit at my little desk, which was barely big enough to fit my expanding butt, and look around thinking that Jackie, Sarah, or anyone else for that matter, couldn't possibly be sneaking tons of food then making themselves throw it all up. I decided they must be the lucky ones, those who simply didn't have to worry about gaining weight or having to eat only certain foods that were good for them. It was clear to me I was different from them, because I had to worry about what foods I ate. I never stopped thinking about which foods were going to make me fatter than I already was. I was preoccupied with what foods I felt I could eat and be okay with and what I would have to purge.

This crazy way of thinking was my secret and now I felt overwhelmed if I didn't have total control over what I was able to eat. I divided food into two primary categories, good foods or bad foods, to make things easier for me. What fell into the good category was safe for me to eat and keep down. Whatever fell into the bad category, I'd purge.

A couple weeks passed and, by accident, I discovered a name for my strange behavior. I was out shopping with my mother one Saturday afternoon and we stopped by the local Danville Thrift store where I bought the first of many workout books. Jane Fonda had written it and there she was, pictured on the cover, resplendent in a leotard and smiling right at me. I felt like she was telling me to pick up the book. I did and thought maybe if I bought the book and followed Jane's instructions, I would lose weight and I wouldn't have to throw up. The book actually provided me with something else. It gave me a medical name for what had now become an everyday occurrence for me. The inside front cover had a section with a small biography of Jane where she mentioned she had once been bulimic. I felt like a light bulb went on when I read that. I understood immediately that when I ate and ate and then threw it all up, I, too, was bulimic.

Jane was older than I was and had recovered from the disease. She was successful too. For starters, she had a published book, workout videos, and was a well-known movie star. When I compared myself to Jane and her accomplishments, I wasn't completely convinced what she described as bulimia was what I had, but it certainly seemed to be the same. Part of me, though, recognized that my attitude and behavior toward food was different. Sure I had discovered the behavior had a name and even a clinical description, but still I wasn't aware of anyone else in my circle engaging in this secret lifestyle. To me the name didn't mean that much, but by now the behavior meant a lot to me—shame. I was far too ashamed to tell anyone my nasty, little secret, and I was humiliated that I had a problem with food. I felt guilty and embarrassed, too fearful to admit to anyone, including my mom, that there was something very wrong with me. I was afraid if anyone found out, they would think I was a freak.

Despite being only thirteen, I sensed eating a ton of food and rushing into the bathroom to put my fingers down my throat to make myself vomit wasn't exactly normal behavior for someone my age. I just couldn't seem to stop. I'd stand in my bedroom alone, staring at myself in the mirror. What I saw looking back was a lonely, hopeless, fat eighth grader. My brown hair was thin and stringy, and my body was large and lumpy in all the wrong places. I was average height. My round face, round and broad shoulders, round belly, and round, pudgy thighs looked to me like a potato, one big, round potato. I thought my only redeeming body part was my calves. For some reason they didn't seem to put on weight like the rest of my body did. Unfortunately for me, the only way I could relieve the emptiness, even for a short time, was with food.

I didn't have anyone I could talk to, even if I mustered up the confidence to do so. I couldn't talk to my mom. She was way too sick and stressed out and even if I'd wanted to talk to my dad, we'd never had a real conversation in all my thirteen years, so he'd be impossible to confide in. Besides, I couldn't risk people thinking I was freaky or, worse, crazy. I wanted to be as invisible as possible and to fit in at school. I knew for certain if I told anyone about my psycho eating ritual, I'd wind up having no friends at all.

I no longer felt like the Jocelyn I once thought I was, but rather, I felt as if I were a stranger living in what was once Jocelyn's body. Food had become the one and only thing I lived for. I focused on food every waking hour of every day, seven days a week. When I sat in class, I'd fantasize about my next meal and when I was home, I'd be planning my next binge.

Food had become not just my obsession but my answer to everything in the was the sole purpose of my existence. Food was my friend and even more importantly, food was my family. I no longer dreamt or fantasized about the future. I thought about the moment, and the moment meant food.

After a couple of months, I was totally out of control. I'd managed to pretend to my family and my friends that everything was great with me and, most importantly, that I was normal. But what I kept inside was the intense sadness at having this freakish, out-of-control addiction to food. I couldn't seem to find a way to stop the obsession from worsening. I knew I needed food to survive and even though I was only thirteen, I knew also that food would ultimately destroy me. The addiction felt so evil. It was revolting to see the self-induced vomit everyday. I concluded I was evil or, at the very least, sick in the head.

Three months into eighth grade, the excitement of being in the most senior class and having the respect it commanded eluded me. All I cared or thought about was how much I weighed. I was fairly smart so I got by in my classes, but food superseded any thoughts of school. My body solely defined who I was, the fat girl, and what I was worth, little to nothing.

I wanted to be a normal thirteen-year-old girl, but I wasn't. I was simply what my outer shell conveyed. The actions of others validated my beliefs. They either commented on my weight or, worse, completely ignored me. When I looked in the mirror, I saw only a fat, lumpy, ugly Jocelyn. When I touched my body, I felt the rolls of skin on my stomach, on my butt, and even on my back. When I listened to people talking, I heard them mention a fat or chubby Jocelyn. I wish I were making this up, but it's true. My family, through their remarks and facial expressions, clearly conveyed that I was overweight. I often saw my dad look at me with embarrassment, especially when we would meet someone in his circle of acquaintances. My mom made no qualms about showing her feelings either. "Jocelyn, I understand if you don't want to go to (this function or that function)." I never heard what I wished to hear, "Jocelyn, you are beautiful and perfect just the way you are."

The kids at school and even complete strangers gave me those funny looks, eyeing me up and down from head to toe in repugnance, or the kids might make a smart remark such as "you pig," while I was eating. I knew I was "big." I'd look around in class everyday and see all the cute, little girls whispering and giggling and wish I looked even remotely like them. But I didn't, no matter how hard I tried or how many times I threw up, hoping for some weight loss miracle.

It pained me every time I came home from school and my mom called out, "Jocelyn, shouldn't you be watching what you're eating?" "Jocelyn, haven't you had enough food?" "Jocelyn, how can you not be full after eating all of that just for a snack?" "Jocelyn, you'll spoil your appetite for dinner if you keep eating." Her comments made me want to crawl into a corner and hide forever.

I wished someone would like me just the way I was. I wanted to feel loved so this sadness would leave for good. I kept hoping, but nothing changed. "Jocelyn, look at your butt. Jocelyn is too heavy for me to go steady with. Jocelyn's gotten fat," echoed in my head for months after my ex-boyfriend, Kurt, said that to me in front of all my friends at school. I could feel my face burning red and everyone staring right at me. Not knowing what to do, I ran to the bathroom to get away and cry. How could Kurt say that to me in front of all those people? He was my first boyfriend, and we'd been together all of last year. Even though we broke up, I thought he had a warm spot in his heart for me. I guessed wrong. He was mean, just like everyone else.

When I wasn't in school, I would hide out alone in my bedroom. I'd usually spend a couple hours lying on my bed pretending I was a different person with a wonderful life. I'd imagine I was skinny, very beautiful, smart, talented, and, of course, popular. I had tons of friends and all the boys liked me. I'd visualize an entirely different family with a mom and dad who were young, energetic, and totally loved spending time with me. I even pretended that I had brothers instead of sisters, thinking they would like hanging out with me, unlike my sisters, both of whom were older.

I knew this was all make-believe, because every night when I pretended I was a princess, I'd cry myself to sleep. The truth is, my life was nothing like my fantasy, and my family didn't act as though they enjoyed spending time with me. My dad never sat down with me and talked about his day or asked me about mine. My sisters were always too busy to spare any time for me. My mom helped me with my homework, but we didn't go out and do fun things together.

When I thought about it, I didn't even feel a part of my family. Rather, I felt more like a lodger who occupied one of the bedrooms in the house. No one had any idea what I did in my room and no one knew how sad I was. I thought if I were someone else and not Jocelyn, or if I were invisible, then I wouldn't have to deal with the constant sadness. Only when I was exhausted from daydreaming or crying or binging and purging could I calm down enough to fall asleep.

I tried to appear as if I were just as normal as anyone else. Like the kids in my grade, I enjoyed spending time after school and on weekends hanging out with my girlfriends. I liked getting away from my house as much as possible and going over to my friends' house to listen to music, watch TV, or hang out with their parents or siblings. It was from spending time at my friend Sandy or Dana's house that I realized how very different my family was. Sandy's and Dana's families all got along and enjoyed having a laugh and spending time together. At least once a year, if not more, they'd go away on vacation together.

My family never went on vacations together. My mom said there was so much screaming and fighting when we were together that it was too stressful for her to go anywhere with the entire family. I recall only one family vacation. We went to Knocti Lake, which was about three hours north of our house, for a few days one summer. I don't remember it being a dreadful experience, but we never took another vacation together. We lived in one of the most visited places in the country, California, yet my parents never took my sisters and me to Disney Land, to Yosemite National Park, the San Diego Zoo, Sea World, or any of the other wonderful places people from the world over came to California to see. We never went to the movies together. After I realized that Knocti Lake would be the only time we'd all go somewhere together, I never asked to do anything. I knew the answer would be some form of no. Instead of expressing my disappointment, sadness, and confusion, I pretended I didn't care and didn't want to do anything together, anyway. I grew used to not enjoying the company of my family.

From that first moment I put my fingers down my throat to make myself throw up all my breakfast, I somehow knew that the experience changed me Gradually, after my episode in the bushes in front of my house, I filled my days preoccupied with my next binge and purge session. Binging and purging became a way for me to feel, to self-comfort, to self-protect, and even to obtain pleasure. What I didn't know was that I would ultimately increase my intense pain by engaging in this behavior. Soon I found myself riding on what seemed to be an endless roller coaster of brief highs followed by deep and protracted lows. Somewhere along the line I lost myself and no longer knew who I was. I only knew I couldn't peacefully co-exist with food, but I couldn't live without it either. What was I going to do? I couldn't stop. I felt like I was slowly dying from the inside out.

Chapter 2

My Blanket of Shadows

It was 1974 and I was nearly seven when my family packed up and moved from upstate New York to California. My dad got a job that promised more money and a better future. The quintessential company man, he jumped at this opportunity.

From as early as I can recall, my dad was never around. He was more involved with his work than with any one of us, especially me. He worked day and night and was on the road traveling more often than he was home. He was always the first to volunteer for any business trip or event. I thought he preferred to get away from our family whenever he could. He spent his entire career faithfully punching in numbers and working more than anyone else to finally achieve the status of VP of Finance, without a college degree. He never took a day off from work until he was in his late sixties. Even our family vacation at Knocti Lake was on a holiday weekend, hence no time away from the office.

We had no relatives living close to us and had no relationship with my dad's immediate or extended family. I assumed my dad cared little for his own family, just like he cared little for us and simply didn't want to mix two families he disliked. My parents didn't have any close friends, either, so moving across the country wasn't a very big deal. My sisters and I were still young enough that starting over wouldn't be too traumatic or difficult. In many ways, we were all looking forward to the warm, sunny weather that California promised.

Since my dad was going to be working in San Francisco, my parents decided we would live just outside the city. Marin County was close enough and not too much of a commute for my dad. It was there, in the city of Tiburon, that my parents bought a beautiful, large, two-story house in an up-and-coming neighborhood. We all had our own bedrooms and bathrooms and the family room was twice the size of any room I had seen before. From nearly everywhere in the house, we had a wonderful view, from the rolling hillside to the beautiful ocean.

This house was perfect. Tiburon was going to be a new beginning for us all. How exciting this time was going to be.

Unfortunately, all that hope and anticipation was just a fleeting illusion. That year and the following years would be pivotal in my life, as everything I thought I knew evaporated and everything I hoped for crashed and burned. I believe this was where I began to change and choose a path of self-destruction as my survival tool. Rather than the storybook existence I'd dreamt about, living in a beautiful home on a beautiful hill overlooking the blue, sparkling ocean, Tiburon ended up being an ugly place for me and my family, one that had a profound effect on everyone.

The new school year began shortly after we all settled in and familiarized ourselves with the town. My two older sisters would be going to the same school, whereas I was still in elementary school. I wasn't any more nervous starting second grade at St. Hillary's Catholic School than I would have been starting any new school year. I was even a little excited about wearing a red, navy, and grey uniform, rather than the plain red and white one I wore back in New York. With excitement and a hint of trepidation, I walked into my new classroom and waited for Sister Bernadette to tell everyone where to sit. Because I was so hopeful this move would bring my family closer together, I also believed that school would be just as promising. As I sat down at my little desk, trying to make myself as comfortable as possible, I looked around to take in my surroundings. The classroom looked pretty much the same as first grade. Learning tools covered the walls, and the more advanced second grade books were neatly stacked. All the girls and boys were friendly and said hello to me.

After a few weeks I made some friends and got along with everyone, even if we didn't play together during recess. My best friend, Jackie, was an only child and had an entirely different family life than I did. Her parents were still in their twenties, unlike mine who were in their forties, and they always did things together. I loved going over to her house to play because it was very different from playing at mine. She had lots of toys and dolls and even a community swimming pool that we splashed around in. Her mom always made us a treat and even her dad would sit with us at night and play cards. I felt calm and peaceful when I was at Jackie's house and was always quick to accept an invitation to spend time there.

My family's fresh start quickly deteriorated and the ugliness would grow with the passing time. My sister, Carolyn, who was six years older than me and Susan who was four years older both attended Del Mar Junior High. We always seemed to be on different pages. Even back in New York, Susan pretty much kept to herself. A natural athlete, she was consumed by the sports she participated in and excelled in all of them. She wasn't home as much as either Carolyn or me, so I knew little about her. We rarely spent time together, although I certainly admired her. She was very bright, even skipped the fourth grade. I always wished I was more like her. Consequently, because she was older than me and participated in sports year round, I thought she wasn't interested in me as a person. I believed I wasn't very important to her, just like everyone else in my family.

On the other hand, I did know a lot about Carolyn. Too much, much more than a seven-year-old should know. Shortly after we all settled into our new home, disturbing events began to unfold in Carolyn's world. She was having a hard time fitting in at Del Mar Junior High and things were no better for her at home. She was ill-equipped to handle the challenges ahead.

Carolyn had suffered mistreatment at the hands of my parents since she was very little. "You're no good. I wish I never had you," my dad used to say to Carolyn when she was not quite seven, according to my mother. "He'd hit and smack her because he was angry," my mom cried. "He did the same to Susan, only not as bad. He just didn't like Carolyn and he made it no secret. But I told him to leave you alone, Jocelyn," and he did—literally.

Any level of parental support via my dad for Carolyn was completely absent. She was subject to constant verbal and physical abuse. It was as if she became the focal point of my dad's inner demons and all his pent-up anger and bitterness.

Carolyn chose to hang with the rougher crowd at school, I believe, because she wanted to feel like she belonged somewhere. Her friends came from a variety of backgrounds. Because of the diversity in their homes, they were more accepting of Carolyn, not uncommon for anyone who doesn't fit the stereotypical child and family. Not surprisingly, she and her new friends were willing to find temporary release and instant pleasure in any way they could. Carolyn began to experiment with drugs. Although only in the eighth grade, her dabbling gave way to excess and the inevitable overdose that followed.

Initially my day started as usual. My mom's tap on my bedroom door awakened me. "Jocelyn, it's time to get up." I donned my school uniform and went to the kitchen to have a bite to eat. Once finished I washed my face and brushed my teeth and waited patiently for my mom to finish getting ready so she could take me to school. The day was unremarkable. I sat at my desk and listened to the lessons Sister Bernadette taught, played with Jackie during recess, and took the bus home after school, just like I did every day. What lay ahead was like walking into someone else's nightmare. As I headed up the hill towards our house, I could see my mom through the kitchen window, looking frantic as she paced back and forth. "Jocelyn, we have no time for a snack. We have to go now," she said with a hysterical tone in her voice. Obeying her as I always did, I got into our burgundy and brown station wagon without a clue as to what was going on or where we were going in such a hurry. We sped away from our house and once we were far enough down the main road, I asked her where we were going. Her answer shocked me. Between her uncontrollable sobs my mom told me she had gotten a call from Carolyn's school and Carolyn had overdosed on pills. *What?* I thought, too afraid to ask any questions. I didn't understand what overdosing meant, but based on the way my mom was falling apart—tears running down her face, her arms and hands shaking as she tried to take hold of the steering wheel—I knew it was serious. Because my mom was hysterical, I became hysterical too. I fed off her emotions and within minutes, I began to cry. Why was she so upset? What was going on? I couldn't understand why she was acting like that in front of me. Within minutes she became confused, making wrong turns and losing her sense of direction. *I don't get it,* I thought. *I'm only seven. Why are you so upset? What is overdosing anyway?* Couldn't she see she was upsetting me? I was disturbed by my mom's reactions and feared she would lose it and we'd crash. Was she going to have a nervous breakdown like the ones I'd seen on TV? What would I do without her? I'd have no one then. *Oh, God, please make everything better.*

Nothing changed as we continued to speed to the school. The only thing I did realize was that the few actual questions I asked evoked no answers. They only added to her hysteria. I decided not to talk anymore, just sit there crying while waiting to see what lay ahead. As we approached the parking lot of Del Mar Junior High, I could make out a small crowd of people gathered around my sister. "Hurry, Jocelyn, get out of the car," my mom shouted over her shoulder, while making a mad dash towards Carolyn.

As I trailed behind my mom, I could hear Carolyn screaming and crying. She was trying to break free from her teachers. Now I knew—because the teachers explained it to my mom as I was standing behind her—that Carolyn had taken a bunch of uppers—some kind of pill—and that's what made her appear crazy. But my mom hadn't taken any pills, so why was she acting crazy too? I was distraught by all the commotion, although right then I was more terrified by the way my mom carried on than how Carolyn did. I knew kids got into trouble. I wasn't that stupid. But my mom, that was a totally different story. Up to that day, I trusted my mom would always be there for me and, aside from her constant battles with illness, she'd always been strong and in control. But seeing her hysterical and forgetting I was witnessing all this by her side frightened me. As the tears streamed down my face, I felt a loss. I no longer had the protection and strength I needed from my mom. I thought I was totally alone.

Eventually after all the screaming and fighting in front of what seemed to be the whole campus, Carolyn was released from the school grounds. We were all free to go home. My mom would have to see her teacher and the principle later, but I cared little about that. I just wanted to get out of there. I was ashamed, embarrassed, and very upset because it was obvious to everyone around that something dreadful was happening. The teachers were upset, the onlookers were staring, Carolyn was distraught, and my mom was a basket case. So much chaos and it wasn't even happening behind closed doors. Does everybody act this way, crazy, screaming, and yelling, not calm and collected, even if a "bad" situation is happening? Couldn't they see that acting this way was just making everything worse? I could. Why couldn't the adults? Sure Carolyn was acting weird, but at least she was more in control—in a funny sort of way—than my mom and the teachers who, I thought, fed off my mom's behavior. Once Carolyn stopped crying, she smiled and laughed. Not my mom, though. She remained frantic, hands and voice still shaking, strange body language, and all alien to me.

During the ride home, as I sat alone in the back seat, I stared at the road beside me, not daring to say a word. Carolyn and my mom barely spoke to each other. My mom was still visibly upset. Carolyn looked back at me several times and smiled. I couldn't help but wonder why my mom took me with her in the first place. Why didn't she phone someone and ask them to take care of me for a while?

No one ever bothered to explain to me what had happened. My mom never came into my room, as I laid on my bed sobbing, to talk with me about the afternoon. I wanted her to tell me everything was going to be okay, she was sorry for frightening me, and she would make everything better. I even hoped if she wasn't going to knock on my bedroom door, then maybe my dad would talk to me when he came home from work. Neither of them ever spoke a word to me about the incident. Instead, I heard them yelling most of the evening at Carolyn and each other. I didn't know what would happen in the end to Carolyn. I tried in vain to shut out the loud noises they were making.

I was trying so hard to be a good little girl. Didn't that count for something? Attention, love, support? But even being a good kid seemed to have little consequence. No one noticed me. When I was cried out, I decided I'd make up my own story as to why my mom and dad didn't care enough about me to see how upset I was from witnessing this event. I decided I'd just pretend that none of it happened, simple as that. I'd somehow convince myself that Carolyn was fine and everything that happened that day was like watching a movie, fake, not real. But I couldn't lie enough to myself to pretend I didn't see my hysterical mom acting like a demented person. That had terrified me so much I started having nightmares.

After that first incident, my mom carted me from place to place to silently witness what seemed like an endless litany of Carolyn's troubles, ones my child's mind could not comprehend. Whenever anything happened with Carolyn, such as a subsequent overdose, my mom always took me along to pick her up. More often than not, Carolyn and my parents were at each other's throats shouting and yelling back and forth over what she did or didn't do. My mom and Carolyn cried, while my dad's tone turned deeper and louder, like he was going to explode. As I quietly observed all the turmoil, I felt more invisible and dislocated from the family.

What I continued to find more disturbing than my sister's getting into trouble was my mom's reactions to these situations. She would become hysterical, and I would ask myself, "What if after one of these situations she gets too upset or, worse, has a breakdown? What will become of me?"

My mom never tried to hide her emotions from me or make up an excuse about these upsetting situations. She never consoled or tried to shelter me. She took me everywhere to witness all the mayhem firsthand. Can't she see how terrified I am? I would ask myself over and over. Why is she bringing me with her? Why am I not important enough to talk to? Why isn't she trying to protect me from all this?

I barely knew Carolyn and now what I did know frightened me to death. As often as possible, I would pretend that none of the things going on were real. Sometimes I could block them out, other times I couldn't. But I could never block out the loneliness, fear, and confusion. When I looked at Carolyn, I felt the pain of another lost child yearning to be loved and never finding it. Every time she reached out for help, comfort, or love, she got a cold shoulder instead. My mother just stood by and watched, enabling this behavior. Many years later I learned in my Marriage and Family class at SDSU, that my dad and mom were abuser/co-enabler in this behavior pattern.

Witnessing this, I was sad, not only for myself but for Carolyn too. Every time I saw her or my mom, they were crying. Not even a year had passed since we'd moved to Tiburon and everything seemed to be going badly for me and my family. It embarrassed and saddened me, so I vowed never to tell Jackie about anything that happened in my home. I worried that if she knew about any of it, she'd no longer be my friend and I needed her friendship. She was different from anyone I knew and treated me with genuine kindness.

At this same time I learned I didn't have the strong, reliable mom I always believed I had. She cried all the time and never stopped worrying about Carolyn or my dad, who simply reacted to all of these situations with increasing rage and anger. I decided it was too awful to contemplate losing whatever I had left of my mom, so I promised myself I wouldn't cause any trouble or make her upset. I knew I had to be an extra good and quiet little girl.

I had never known my dad and now that the main focus was on Carolyn, he had absolutely no time for me. For the first time in my life, I wished I had a different dad, one like Jackie's, perhaps, because I needed to feel loved and protected. Instead, I grew increasingly afraid of my real dad. He seemed to live eternally on the cusp of rage, ready for a battle at any moment and at the slightest perceived provocation. I learned to fear his red, glowering face, and the way his body would grow stiff and rigid with pent-up anger. His behavior, along with my mom's fragile health, made me recoil and spend as much time as I could alone in my room, away from all the chaos. I was learning how to comfort myself without my parent's help.

Just when I thought things couldn't get any worse, they did. My mother and I were driving down the main highway in Tiburon. I was sitting in the passenger seat watching the sun sparkle off the road ahead of me when she panicked. In a split second, she'd lost control of herself and told me she couldn't see clearly. "What?" I asked her.

"All the lanes are blurry, Jocelyn. I don't know which one is the right lane and which is in my imagination." I was horrified. I didn't know how to drive. I thought we were going to die. I started to cry. My mom asked me to guide her so we could get home right away. I had to concentrate. Somehow I pulled myself together and managed to direct us home to safety.

She went to the hospital afterwards and the doctors discovered she had had a Multiple Sclerosis, or MS, attack while she was driving. My worst fears were coming true. My mom was now extremely ill and had to stay in the hospital while the doctors did all kinds of tests and helped her as best they could. I felt my heart collapse, as though it had literally fallen down into my stomach. Now I had nobody. I had become somewhat accustomed to seeing her hysterical time and again, but now that she had a disease, I lost all hope for a happy family life. I understood only that my mom was going to be away for a while because she was very sick. Because my dad worked all day and my sisters were at school the same as I was, my next door neighbor would take care of me.

Linda was a jolly, large lady with a warm and loving personality. She volunteered to pick me up from school and take me to her house until someone came home to care for me. She made an effort to make me feel good. Everyday after she picked me up and we went back to her house, she would have some type of homemade sweet, cake, or pastry for me to eat. She'd sit down with me at the kitchen table and ask me about my day before helping me with my school lessons. Then I'd watch TV until someone knocked on her door to let me know I could go home.

I appreciated Linda's kindness, but day by day I grew sadder and lonelier. Everything at home was falling apart right in front of me, and nobody cared enough about me to explain what MS was or how it would affect my mom and the rest of us. I had no idea if it was just a sickness that would go away or if it would stay forever. Not knowing whether my mom was going to die was worse than any of those thoughts. I started to feel even more isolated and began trying to figure out how I would survive on my own.

When my mom finally returned from the hospital, I was shocked by her appearance. The MS attack had resulted in her inability to control the right side of her body. A brace covered her arm and she wore a black patch over her right eye. When she saw the alarmed look on my face, she explained she had to wear the brace to keep her arm from shaking uncontrollably. She went on to tell me her perception was temporarily damaged, just like it had been when she had the attack in the car, and the eye patch would help until her double vision cleared up.

I wasn't prepared for this. I had anxiously waited for my mom to come home and thought she would be like her old self, otherwise the doctors wouldn't let her come back home. I was mistaken. When I first saw her, I was completely devastated and sadder than I had ever been. I could see how sick she was. I knew then that everything wasn't going to go back to being like it was before. Now that I understood the gravity of her situation, I promised myself I would do my best to never put any pressure whatsoever on my mom. I believed she was too weak physically and emotionally to handle any more stress. I vowed I wouldn't get into any trouble for as long as I lived.

I began expressing my sadness through my body because I was so unhappy and felt like I had no one to turn to for support. Every school day, I'd walk up to Sister Bernadette's desk staring down at the floor and tell her I wasn't feeling well. She would send me to the nurse's office where I could lie down on a cot. Like clockwork, I became nauseous every day at the same time. Only when I was alone lying on the little cot was I able to cry, and then afterwards I'd feel some relief.

Although I never spoke about how sad my mom's illness made me, I knew being alone during the middle of the day allowed me to somehow sort through or, more likely, bury my sorrow. I desperately hoped that someone, Sister Bernadette or one of the nurses, would come and talk with me or, even better, tell me everything was going to be fine. No one did. My teacher and the school nurse both smiled at me every afternoon as I walked out of class and down the hallway straight for the backroom where the cold, sheet-covered cot waited for me. I couldn't make sense of the realities of my mom's illness or how I was supposed to feel, let alone understand it all. Instead, I went to lie down every day for the next couple months and avail of the strange comfort the isolation provided me.

Chapter 3

A Thousand Shades of Black

Our first year in California had passed and whatever hopes we all entertained had not materialized. Nothing went right for anyone that year, and my dad and mom believed we all needed a change.

Susan's diving had progressed and she had found a very good, well-known diving school she wanted to attend in Lafayette, which was located in the East Bay. She was starting to show exceptional talent and winning most all her competitions. Although Susan experienced some of the physical abuse that Carolyn did, she found an escape by immersing herself in extra-curricular activities. In many ways she adopted the behaviors of my dad, but where he was involved with his job, she fixated on sports to the exclusion of everything at home. She took every activity lesson she could. Other than the odd engagement in some type of sport such as ice-skating, Susan and I did very little together. She found comfort in the fast-paced environment of sports and the intensity of scholastics.

Susan's diving needs provided a perfect excuse to move away from Marin County, start anew, and forget the traumatic year in Tiburon. My parents agreed East Bay would be convenient enough for my dad to commute to San Francisco to work and they hoped it would be a better place to raise the three of us. With that, Carolyn's misfortunes at school, and my mom's MS diagnosis in mind, my parents zeroed in on the town of Alamo for our new home. They looked at a number of different houses in various neighborhoods, and then chose one located on a little side street off Alamo's main road. They decided on that particular house because it was important to them not to live too close to any neighbors. My mom told me she didn't want anyone in our new neighborhood to hear all the shouting and screaming that emanated nonstop from our home. She also told me, many years later, she didn't want to face the embarrassment if anyone were to learn how terribly we conducted ourselves behind closed doors.

At the time I didn't know why they chose that particular house and couldn't understand why we didn't buy one of the many other beautiful homes we could well afford in a nicer, more prestigious neighborhood. But in 1975, with Carolyn in complete disarray and me quiet as ever and with no discussion or choice, we moved into the two-story, Tahoe-style house with brownish-red wood on the outside and brown paneling covering most every wall inside.

Our new home slumbered on Austin Lane. Those wishing to venture forth encountered two bridges and three bumps before turning into our driveway. The neighborhood itself was very small, just one little bumpy road with cracks and potholes every few feet, and the overall impression it gave was one of weirdness. An abundance of huge, overhanging trees darkened the neighborhood more than any of the others where we had house-hunted. Each of the twenty or so houses on the street was secluded and creepy in its own unique way such as the one that had sheets covering the windows rather than curtains. I imagined that every one held its own dark secrets and later it turned out that my childish imagination was not entirely wrong. There were more strange people with bizarre stories than not living on our little lane, which came nowhere close to looking like any of the modern neighborhoods in Alamo. In fact the oldest house in all of Alamo sat right on the top of our little lane, as did the second and third oldest houses, which added to the sense of decay emanating from the neighborhood.

I switched schools for the fourth time since starting my formal education. I now was going to attend St. Isidore's Catholic School in Danville. My eighth birthday was in late September, and I was starting the third grade. This time starting all over made me nervous. I didn't know anyone, and I didn't know if anyone would want to be friends with me. I missed my best friend, Jackie, back at St. Hillary's, and wished I was going to the third grade there.

When the school year started, I had no major problems and adjusted fairly quickly. I didn't make any immediate friends but I managed to spend recess and lunch in the playground, playing with the other kids in my class. I didn't like the nun who was my teacher, Sister Mary. I felt like she wasn't very nice to me. She spoke with a bitter tone all the time and never seemed happy about anything. Nearly every day from the first day I walked into her classroom, she'd scold me in front of the whole class, shouting that I was writing incorrectly and holding my pencil the wrong way. I could see that ignorant Lewis, who sat beside me, crack up every time Sister Mary approached my desk. He was the class suck-up and always did everything "right." I, however, did everything "wrong," according to Sister Mary. Instead of using only my index finger to guide the pencil when I wrote, I used both my index finger and middle finger. At Saint Hillary's the way I held my pencil wasn't a concern as long as I did the work, so I didn't understand why Sister Mary made it an issue. Her perseverance prevailed, and I ended up with a permanent red bump on my middle finger without producing any more brilliant or insightful writing than I had before her ill-conceived intervention.

During my first year at St. Isidore's my family made one vain attempt at addressing the serious issues that afflicted us by going to family therapy. I would leave class mid-morning and head off with my entire family in our station wagon for a therapy session at the hospital in Walnut Creek. I was embarrassed going to therapy because when I returned, the kids would ask where I'd been. I would get flustered, not wanting to tell the truth, and make up something such as a doctor or dentist appointment.

What disturbed me more than lying to the kids in my class was our lack of progress during the sessions. When we all first arrived at John Muir Hospital Therapy Unit, the counselor told us the purpose of these meetings was to provide a safe place for us to come together and express our feelings openly. She could then help us resolve them. A nice theory, but instead of everyone sharing and expressing their feelings in this controlled environment, my parents and sisters attacked each other like wild animals. Within just a few minutes of arriving, everyone was screaming and yelling at each other. It was all-out warfare.

I adopted the role of the unseen observer, sitting on the sidelines in silence. Chaos and emotions flew everywhere as the combatants grew angrier, more bitter, and more entrenched by the minute. I was stunned. I thought the whole reason they dragged me out of my classroom was to fix the family, make it like a normal family. Realizing that, as usual, I was invisible to everyone, I'd simply focus on the wall clock when the going got too brutal for me to endure and watch the big hand move until the hour was over.

I'd come out of these sessions feeling worse about myself and my unhappy family. I would go back to class after lunch and pretend to the kids I was fine. I'd smile and try to focus on whatever distraction I could find. I was getting good at putting on a brave face, a talent that served me well in subsequent years, but on the inside I ached about the reality that nobody in my family seemed to notice or care about me. My mom, dad, Carolyn, and Susan were so fixated on each other that no one noticed me. I hoped the counselor would make them pay attention to me but she didn't. I was just a silly kid in the corner, yet they had insisted I be there. It didn't make sense to me. It may have been they were so used to dragging me along everywhere that they had simply forgotten what was appropriate for a child of my age and what impact all of this was having on me. The mayhem would continue in the car afterwards and, as with most things in my family, it was a short-lived project that was soon abandoned. Even at such a young age, I could see the therapist was in over her head and couldn't control the situation.

My first year in Alamo at St. Isidore's Catholic School, just like back in Tiburon, was a great disappointment. Loneliness was my constant companion. On top of the total chaos at home and my daily humiliation by Sister Mary, I had also started to become self-conscious about my body. This manifested itself after I had begun to try and understand, as best as an eight-year-old could, why my family ignored me or didn't think I was important. Was it because I was dumb? No, I wasn't dumb. I wasn't a star pupil, but I knew I was pretty good, above average. Was it because I was mean and obnoxious? No way, I barely said anything unkind. If I did, I'd feel so guilty I'd end up crying. The only thing left was the fact I was beginning to put on weight. I concluded it must be because I was getting fat. Neither Carolyn nor Susan was fat. They were both pretty skinny, especially Carolyn who, if anything, was underweight. I deduced I wasn't skinny enough and pretty enough, otherwise everything would be different. That was it, I'd figured it out.

Once I decided that I wasn't beautiful and had a round body, especially my torso, I started to look around my class and take note of what the other girls looked like. Christy was cute. She was small and peppy. Her mom loved her. She was always doing things for her. And Cheryl was tall and very skinny. She played with her two sisters all the time, and it didn't matter that her oldest sister, Dena, was four years her senior, just like my sister Susan. So at eight, I believed I was not worthy of real relationships or attention because I was fat and ugly.

This realization coincided with the end of the school year. I breathed a sigh of relief to be delivered from Sister Mary and glad I didn't have to wear a fake smile and pretend I was happy. Above all, I was glad I could avoid being surrounded by all the skinny, cute girls at St Isidore's, even if it was only for the summer.

Chapter 4

The Invisible Child

I first learned how to swim when I was four. We lived in Syracuse, New York, within walking distance of an indoor pool. Both Carolyn and Susan knew how to swim and once I was old enough, I wanted to learn too. I was a natural and in no time I was good enough to join the swim team and compete in races. I fell in love with the sport and because I showed a real talent for it, I remained passionate and involved, swimming competitively for the next fourteen years. During my first years as a swimmer, I was always thrilled to be in the water, swimming as fast as I could and racing from one end of the pool to the other. For years, I loved the sensation of freedom that floating in the blue water brought me. As the water splashed around me, I lived in the moment and forgot all my problems. Nothing else came close to giving me that peaceful, serene feeling. I was immediately hooked and knew I'd be a swimmer for life.

Unfortunately, as I began to get older, my attitude towards my most precious sport began to change. I had reveled in the momentary joy and freedom swimming provided me and usually won every race I entered. I especially loved swimming the breast stroke and back stroke. They were my favorites and the ones at which I excelled. But, like all girls my age, my body began to change. My mom and I had never talked about bodies changing or what growing up entailed, so this completely petrified me. Panicking, I'd think, I'm already chubby, am I going to get even bigger? Why is everything growing? I was far too embarrassed to admit my worries to anyone and knew that my sisters wouldn't understand because they were skinny. This wasn't a subject I wanted to talk about with my dad and even if I had, he'd be less than useless. My mom already had too much on her plate for me to share my fears with her. I was left hoping that, miraculously, I'd awaken some morning and all my new bulges would be gone.

My family had a membership at Round Hill Country Club so my sisters and I could use the pool and facilities. One warm, sunny August afternoon, Round Hill's swim team members were wandering about or flopping on the chairs, chaise lounges, and on the grass, waiting to compete against Northgate High. They had a great team, one of the best in the Bay Area, with fast, talented swimmers. This competition would determine whether anyone on the Round Hill and Northgate teams would make qualifying times to compete in the county meet. Only the best swimmers would make it.

All my team friends had their families, even grandparents, there, cheering them on, picnic baskets filled with sandwiches and sodas. My mom was the only one in my family who came to watch. As I waited for my heat to come, I got more and more nervous. I felt uncomfortable around so many people. My mom's presence helped only a little. Seeing all the kids from Round Hill hanging out in their little circles created a tense feeling inside me. Rather than making a good time, I worried that people would notice only my Mom was with me. The tension built until I had butterflies in my stomach. Moments later, without warning, I accidentally soiled my swimsuit right in front of the whole gathering. I cried uncontrollably, mortified, as my mom rushed me to the bathroom where I could wash myself. I covered up the best I could with the few items we'd brought with us before I had to stand, wearing only a swimsuit, on the podium where everyone would notice the brown stain on my bottom. I wanted to go home, but wasn't willing to give up this moment I had worked so hard for and that would determine whether I would go to the big meet.

"Swimmers take your mark." The gun popped and I swam as fast as I could, moving my arms and legs like I was swimming for my life. I knew the harder I swam, the more I'd splash, giving myself a better chance of achieving a good time and also washing away the brown stain on my butt. I did it. I made qualifying time. I'd go to the County meet and best of all, given my mishap, I could also go home now. I had achieved my best race time ever but it didn't feel like anything to me. The whole experience was overwhelming and the sooner I got home to the lonely sanctuary of my bedroom, the better.

That night during dinner, my dad and sisters finally congratulated me, but by then it just didn't mean much to me. There was no enthusiasm in their voices and more importantly, I couldn't get past the fact they hadn't come to watch me even though they knew how important this meet was. It was a Saturday. Surely they could have come if they wanted. They didn't, and I didn't bother to tell them how I felt. It wouldn't have mattered anyway. I was getting used to being disappointed.

The season for swim team was coming to an end. Since only a few people were competing in the big race, the coaches decided to have the awards dinner beforehand. I stood an excellent chance at winning Most Valuable Player. I was very excited, especially because swimming was the only thing I felt I excelled in. Everyone on the team looked forward to the evening.

I decided I'd wear my favorite outfit, cream and tangerine summer dress with big bows on the shoulders and my favorite white sandals. I spent an extra long time brushing my hair and putting my barrettes in just the right places. I knew it would be an exciting night as I was nearly a hundred percent positive that of all the girls in my group, I was the one who was going to get a trophy.

As I walked into the kitchen to wait for us all to go to the night's big event, I discovered that only my mom and Carolyn were going with me. I was devastated. Time after time, I'd watched all the parents, sisters and brothers, and even grandparents come to the races, sometimes attending the practices as well, but mine never did. And time after time, I pretended I didn't care and would make a conscious effort to be in the pool either swimming or just splashing around so no one would notice the disappointment I felt. But tonight was different. It was supposed to be my biggest night ever, but neither my dad nor Susan cared. I had built this night up so much in my mind and, before the event even began, my heart sank and the excitement evaporated.

The three of us went, and I did win the MVP trophy. I came home with the most important prize anyone could win, but it had already become just a hard piece of metal to me. My dad patted my back as he passed me on his way out and offered cursory congratulations. Even my success hadn't enticed him to take an interest.

As usual, my parents were far too occupied with either themselves or my older sisters to notice how their lack of support upset me. Nothing changed over the years and all their spare time and energy was mainly devoted to my sisters. This just continued to reinforce my diminishing self-worth and reasoning that my physical appearance was to blame. By the ripe old age of nine, I felt like an outsider in my own family. I figured if swimming didn't attract their attention, then their lack of interest must be directly related to the fact that I was too fat for them. I assumed they must be embarrassed or ashamed to be with a fat kid like me. My outer shell now seemed too big for the scared little girl I felt was hiding on the inside. My self-perception of an imperfect body began to inform all my thoughts and soon became my explanation for everyone's attitude toward me.

When I started fourth grade, I was still attending St. Isidore's and knew all the kids. I wasn't quite as nervous as I had been starting the previous year and just had the typical first-day jitters. This year proved to be better for me than the third grade—at least on the academic side. I also made more friends and enjoyed myself more in school. My best friend that year, and for several more years to follow, Monica, and I shared a mutual dislike towards each other the year before. We rarely spoke to one another in third grade and when we did, it was usually with a nasty tone. Somehow we became friends, and I was delighted because I had a lot of fun with her. We hung out together at school and on the weekends, and soon became inseparable.

Everything was going well when I was traumatized by a disturbing event I could never have seen coming. Another classmate, Maria, had invited me to sleep over at her house. I always loved taking advantage of any opportunity that allowed me to spend time away from my home. I was excited about potentially having another friend and looked forward to the evening.

When Friday finally arrived, I went directly to Maria's after school. She lived in one of the very private communities in Danville, where nearly all the homes were large and some even had horse stables. Huge willow trees cast shadows everywhere, hiding the houses, and the secrets within, from one another. I was a little overwhelmed when I first walked in the front door. It was much larger than my house and even had a playroom solely for Maria and her siblings. I didn't know such rooms existed.

Maria showed me around and we had a snack, then decided to play some board games. Although I was intimidated by her siblings, especially her brother because I didn't have one and wasn't used to being around an older boy, I did my best to appreciate her hospitality. As the night drew to an end, I found it rather strange that we weren't going to sleep in her room, especially because she had two separate beds in it. I didn't want to be rude or spoil my chances of being invited back, so I said nothing and pretended to be excited about sleeping under only a few blankets in a spare room.

Maria and I built a cozy little nest where we'd sleep. I fluffed my pillow and lay down beside her, thinking we'd just talk until we dozed off. What happened moments later was so horrific for me that I blocked it out for nearly twenty-two years. Within minutes of making ourselves warm and comfortable, Maria changed the subject of our conversation and started to ask me questions such as, "Have you looked at yourself down there?" "Have you touched yourself down there?" "Has anyone touched you there?"

I froze. I didn't know what to say. I could feel panic rising and I wanted to scream so everyone in her family would come running to my rescue, but I was too afraid. What was Maria saying? Why was she suddenly talking like this to me and what was she going to do? I was more frightened than I had ever been before. I wanted to be home in my own bed, alone. At nine, I was still too naïve to know what Maria meant by touching. I'd never thought about my private parts, let alone talked about them. I knew this wasn't good. I sensed something terrible was going to happen.

With all my willpower, I held back my tears while Maria told me to pull up my pajama top. Her personality changed right in front of me. No longer just another little girl, she took on a more grown-up, sinister demeanor. She said she wanted to see me and that she would let me see her. What? No, this wasn't what I thought a sleepover was supposed to be. My mind was paralyzed and although I wanted to resist, I couldn't. Maria was so strong and overpowering. I pulled my pajama top up to my neck as Maria told me to do. But it didn't end there. As sweat began to cover my forehead and drip down my back, Maria insisted I pull down my pajama bottoms.

Now I was scared. I wanted to wake up and find this to be nothing but a nightmare. It was real, though, and it was happening. Maria pulled off her pajama bottoms and took my hand and placed it on her private parts. She even insisted on guiding me down there, telling me to explore her. I wanted to throw up. I felt sick. My hand was shaking uncontrollably. I felt vile and disgusting. I looked up at her and a strange smile crept across her face as if she were enjoying my frightened touch.

Then Maria put her hand in my pajama bottoms. I was rigid and unable to resist when she moved it down onto my private parts. I closed my eyes and prayed to God to make all this go away. I was beyond terrified and felt like a dirty little girl. Maria touched me and talked to me at the same time, asking in a strange voice if I liked what she was doing. I didn't answer. I froze in silence, waiting for her to stop. Once Maria took her hand off me, I quickly fixed my pajamas and curled up in a little ball, pretending to fall asleep. I waited and waited for the night to turn into day. I couldn't sleep a wink. I couldn't stop thinking about what had just happened. I was so ashamed that I promised myself I would never tell anyone about it. Once daybreak came, I ran to the bathroom, washed myself with a tissue and some soap, and put on my clothes. As soon as we finished breakfast, I asked to use the phone to call my mom to come and get me.

I didn't care if Maria or her mom thought it was rude that I wanted to leave right after eating. I had to get out of there as soon as possible. My mom came shortly after I phoned her, and I raced out the front door to our station wagon. As my mom and Maria's mom chatted, I stared blankly at the dashboard and didn't say anything other than "thank you" to my hostesses. I was focused on going home where I could run to my room and be alone. Although I had promised myself I wouldn't tell anyone about that night, I secretly hoped, in vain as it turned out, that my mom would notice something was wrong. She asked if I had a good time, and then we drove home in silence. As soon as I entered our house, I went straight to my room and locked the door.

Although I didn't fully understand the night before and why Maria made me engage in such a horrible act, I knew it wasn't right for her to have forced me into it. But I convinced myself if anyone found out about it, they would think I was dirty and would blame me. If anyone in my class found out, I was afraid they would tease me and I'd have no friends to play with. I laid on my bed hoping and praying that Maria wasn't going to blab to anyone at school about what happened. If she did, I could lie and call Maria a liar, but I wasn't convinced who our friends would believe. Much to my relief, the following Monday at school Maria didn't mention it to anyone. I tried subtly avoiding her but not enough for her to notice, get angry, and tell people.

Several weeks passed with no incident, but then Maria approached me in the schoolyard and asked me to a sleep over again. Monica, Tim, Stacey, and most of the kids in my class were around us. Dumbfounded, I didn't know what to say. I accepted her invitation. I had only three days to figure out what to do. As each day passed, I couldn't come up with a reason to cancel. I didn't feel I could go back and tell my mom what had happened. She already had too many problems to deal with, which was all she ever spoke to me about. I didn't want to be responsible for making her sicker than she was or for causing her to have one of the episodes I had witnessed with Carolyn.

Reluctantly, I packed my sleepover bag and, after classes finished, got into the backseat of Maria's family's brown station wagon and headed off to her dreadful house in the upscale community just fifteen minutes from St. Isidore's. The willow trees now took on a more sinister appearance and confirmed to me that they did, indeed, help keep dark secrets away from prying eyes. As I walked through the front door, I instantly felt an overwhelming sense of panic. Was this night going to be like the last time? I played cards with her in the family room alongside her brother and dad. After dinner—I could barely eat anything—her mom told us to watch TV before getting ready for bed. Okay, I thought to myself, tonight will be different. Maybe that was just a very bad experience, a one-off. Maybe Maria regrets it as much as I do.

Still uncomfortable in the presence of her brother, we all watched TV together until about nine o'clock. Then her mom walked into the family room and told us to get ready for bed. I could feel myself becoming panicky. Where were we sleeping? How could I ask Maria to sleep in her room, where there were two beds, instead of the spare room? I was tongue-tied. While I changed in her bathroom,

Maria got the same blankets and pillows as the previous time. Then I knew—tonight would be like last time.

I didn't want to cry or make a fool of myself in front of her entire family, so I followed Maria with my blanket and pillow to the spare room. Within about a half hour, Maria proceeded to make the same requests. This time, I pretended that it was all a dream, that it wasn't happening, and it was just an awful nightmare. I said nothing, didn't answer any of her questions, and remained stiff and unyielding.

My complete detachment worked. Afterward, Maria became irritated and told me to follow her into her room. She promptly got into her bed and, pointing to the other one said, "You sleep there."

I turned my back to her so she couldn't see the tears running down my cheeks. Why did she do this to me? I was glad it was over, but now I feared her anger with me might cause her to tell out of spite. Then I'd get into big trouble. My mom would get even sicker and my dad might get mad at me, like he did with Carolyn and Susan. Why did I say yes to a sleepover? Why didn't I make up an excuse? I lay there crying, with that familiar feeling that I'd somehow brought this on myself.

The only thing I could think to do now was to make sure Maria never got another chance to do this to me. I didn't want to be her friend, and I never wanted to set foot in that awful house again. Just like the time before, I knew I couldn't tell my mom the full story. I told her I didn't want to play with Maria anymore. I was hoping my mom would ask me why, but she never did. I was even sadder because she didn't notice I was upset. Or maybe she did and just didn't care. The whole ordeal was so horrific for me that I remained in a constant state of panic for months after. I was afraid someone would find out and I would be labeled dirty and not worthy of friendship. Still, I managed to avoid Maria and said almost nothing to her for the rest of the school year. At least I was successful in keeping her at bay.

As time passed, I managed to bury and forget the events of those two nights. It wasn't until I was in my thirties when I ran into Maria's mom at my local pharmacy that those dormant memories come flooding back. I was in the Blackhawk Longs Drugs wanting to scream at her and tell her what happened. I was tempted to ask her what the hell had been going on in her house, because a nine-year-old learns that behavior from somewhere. I was instantly infuriated with her because I had buried those horrible experiences with the intention of never revisiting them. She had opened an emotional door for me that I'd been quite happy to keep closed. My hurt and anger manifested not just towards Maria's mom but my mom as well. I was angry because my mom never asked me why I no longer wanted to be friends with Maria. She never noticed the terror in my eyes or the desperate tone in my voice when I phoned her to pick me up.

After running into Maria's mom that day, I told my mother about the incident with Maria. She responded, "I was wondering why you told me you no longer wanted to be friends with Maria." Just like she did with everything significant to me, she dismissed that traumatic event with her trite remark. At least I could take comfort in the fact that by that point, I was smart enough to address these resurrected memories and feelings in my therapy and not leave them unresolved.

Chapter 5

House of Shadows

My transformation into a pre-teen was apparent—the changes in my ten-year-old body, especially my weight gain, were overwhelming. I felt terribly insecure about my looks. Around that time, I discovered the scale in the corner of my parent's bathroom and decided to weigh myself. I was neither tall nor short for my age, but what the scale read, seventy-five pounds, shocked me. I thought seventy-five pounds was too much for a fifth grader to weigh. I convinced myself that no one I knew could possibly weigh that much. It didn't matter, anyway, because I could feel the rolls of blubber on my stomach. I looked back at the little white scale as I walked out. I went straight to my room, closed the door, and stared into space, trying to forget what the scale said I weighed.

As the week passed, I tried my best to watch what I ate. While lunching in the school cafeteria, I would eat just the same amount of food as Monica, who was thin, so I wouldn't gain weight. I figured if I ate like her, then maybe the next time I got on the scale it would tell me I'd lost weight. Next time I got on, however, nothing had changed. The same number registered. Emotionally, I felt beaten up because I trusted that if I followed Monica and secretly ate what she ate, then I'd surely lose weight.

This incident started a lifelong love-hate relationship with the scales. Because I was becoming more and more concerned with my weight, whatever the scale indicated directly affected my perception of myself. Those loathsome numbers determined how I felt that day. If I lost a pound, I was happy. If I gained a pound, I was upset. What started as curiosity turned into compulsion.

My insecurity manifested in many ways and thoughts. Appearance ranked number one in terms of determining my level of self-worth, and I believed everyone else's as well. Next in line was how horrible a person and how horrible a sinner I believed I was. Being raised a Catholic and attending Catholic schools meant constant lessons in guilt and unworthiness reinforced spectacularly by my mom, who considered everything a sin and never missed an opportunity to let me know I was committing many of them.

"Jocelyn, you know that using God's name in vain is a mortal sin." "Jocelyn, if you think bad thoughts, it is a sin." "Jocelyn, you have to confess all your sins to the priest in confession or it's another sin." When I studied religion in class, I wondered why my mom and the nuns never told me anything good about God, why they focused only on sinful actions and consequences. Neither they nor my mom ever shared a happy story describing a loving God or saints and angels or even children's favorites such as "Noah's Ark." Instead, we learned about the commandments, especially "Thou Shalt Not Use the Lord's Name in Vain" and "Honor Thy Father and Mother."

Far worse than committing an actual sin was the fact that I apparently could go to hell if I didn't confess them and truly repent for committing them. I knew that I was a sinner—my mom, my school, and my faith told me so. Sometimes I swore, used God's name in vain, and even yelled. Undoubtedly I was bad. I knew God would punish me by sending me straight to hell when I died, because to my child's mind, everyone around me considered using God's name in vain a serious sin, almost as serious as murder! This fear of going to Hell began to increase and cause me to have panic attacks every month when I had to pay a visit to the priest for confession. My intense fear became so overwhelming that every fourth Saturday of the month, when my mom announced we were going to confession before mass, I couldn't eat the entire day prior to that horrible deadline. If I did chance eating anything, toast or maybe a bowl of Rice Krispies, inevitably my stomach would cramp to the point I would end up with diarrhea.

"Jocelyn, don't worry, I had the same problem when I was a little girl. Only then, I had to walk a mile one way to get to confession. Because I was nervous, I'd have to turn around and go home to use the toilet and then walk all the way back to church to go to confession." This was my mom's way of making me feel better. It was fine to her, entirely acceptable, that I had been reduced to a nervous wreck with diarrhea. To her, this meant I was taking my religion seriously. Each month brought on a new level of frenzy when I'd have to go into that little, dank-smelling confessional booth and tell the strange, dark silhouette all the terrible things I had done over the previous four weeks.

This cycle of stress and intense nervousness got so bad I convinced myself if I forgot to tell the priest all my sins, God wouldn't forgive me and, ultimately, I would go to hell where I'd burn forever in a cauldron of fire. One day I decided the best way to ensure my redemption was to write all my sins on a piece of paper. That way, when I went into the confessional booth, knelt down, and divulged all my horrible sins, I could just read from my sheet of paper and not forget to tell the priest everything. What I thought was a brilliant idea turned into a confession session I'd never forget.

That Saturday, at half past three sharp, my mom and I stood in line with all the other "sinners" at St Isidore's Church, patiently waiting our turn to confess. "Oh, God, please don't make me have to go into the booth with the glass door where everyone can see. Please let one of the solid-door rooms be available next so I can go inside one of them instead," I prayed in silence. My stomach began to ache now and the palms of my hands were sweating profusely. The light above the glass door went off. That meant the person who had just confessed his sins would be leaving and I'd have to use that booth. Everyone would see my back. I wouldn't be hidden like in the other one.

I had no choice. Off I went to kneel down on the little brown stool and wait for the priest to open the little window and speak. "Bless me, Father, for I have sinned. It's been a month since my last confession," I began reciting.

"Yes, what have you to say?" I took the tiny folded piece of paper I had placed into the right pocket of my tan pants and unfolded it as fast as I could, knowing if anyone was looking into the room where I knelt, they could see me and my sheet of paper. I tried to keep it directly in front of me as I read my list of sins to the priest. He interrupted in the midst of my reading and told me to stop. What? Am I that bad? I thought. What's going to happen now?

He launched into a litany of how horrible it was that I had written my sins on a piece of paper. His angry tone was getting harder and meaner—it felt to me like he was softly shouting—and I could smell his stale breath coming through the metal grill as he repeated over and over how terrible what I had done was. I wanted to run out of there as fast as I could, but what would my mom think? What would everyone who was in the church think?

I couldn't leave. Not only did I have to stay and let him finish scolding me, but also I had to attend mass afterwards. Looking back now, I have to wonder what satisfaction he could have drawn from bullying a child who was obviously trying to be conscientious. The way he and the others presented religion was so warped it rendered the answer—if there was one—meaningless. For my penance, he told me to recite three Our Fathers and three Hail Mary's and five Glory Be's, more than anyone had ever given me for my sins. I figured my efforts at being thorough had only made me look worse in God's eyes.

I left the confessional, totally deflated. I felt like I couldn't even confess my sins the right way. I was bad, a failure, ashamed of myself. I couldn't concentrate at all the following hour as my mom and I sat through mass. I thought only of the priest and how mean and angry he sounded with me. I wanted to go home and eat. I was hungry and needed to feel some level of comfort as now, more than ever, I was convinced Hell had a spot reserved for me.

As time passed with no change in my relationship with my family, I became increasingly prone to hiding my feelings, whether they were of joy or sorrow. I didn't feel valued as a member of my family, and no one bothered to notice. My dad and I still hadn't done anything together, not even tossed a ball in the back yard, yet he spent a lot of time with my sisters, especially Susan. It was obvious she was his favorite. He was always at her diving school and attended as many competitions as he could. I didn't understand why I wasn't important to him and assumed it was because I was fat and I wasn't pretty.

My mom's and my relationship was different. I had fully accepted that only when she was not spending time dealing with the latest family saga or not feeling too sick would she spend any time with me. I was sad when I started to realize this, especially back in Tiburon, but in Alamo I started to get used to it, expect it even. I was grateful for the small amount of time she spent helping me with my homework, but I yearned for her to play with me, too, as I had never played a sport with her or done any physical activity with her. I knew it was because she was too sick and depressed, but the sense of loss was acute. Sometimes when my mom tucked me in bed at night, I would hope that maybe she'd tell me stories about her childhood, but she never did … in retrospect, I can understand why.

My mom's family had its own set of dysfunctional behaviors. Her father died when she was seventeen as she sat on his lap talking with him. She was closer to her dad than her mom, and how she came to deal with this loss, I don't know. Her mother was less than kind to her. She used to call her horse mouth, would often tell her she was chubby, and, overall, never made her feel like she was good enough. She forced religion down my mother's throat, instilling the fear of God in her. To this day, my mother wrongly believes she didn't repeat this with her own children but, rather, tried to do the opposite. Overall her family was extremely religious, so much so that her mom sent her only two brothers off to study to become priests when they turned fifteen. Her only sister, nine years her junior, was the favorite, according to my mom. She and my mom remain friendly to this day and talk often, yet as a child, I recall only seeing them together once or twice.

I wanted my mother to explain the problems in our family and understand for a moment the impact those problems were having on me. I wanted her to look at me and discover the secret life I lived and reach out and drag me back from the depths to which I had plummeted. Instead, she seemed relieved that I was not as much trouble as the others and left it at that, furthering her dysfunctional legacy.

That year would prove to be a very important time in terms of recognizing my own family dynamics. In some ways, I felt older than my actual age of ten, especially because I had seen and lived through so many traumas in my family life. Every time I visited Monica or even one of my neighbors' homes, I could sense how they all interacted so differently from our family. When their dads came home from work, they'd hug their kids and give them a kiss on the cheek, happy to see them and their wives. Sometimes, their dads would hang out with us and ask us to tell him about our day, something my dad never did. Their moms smiled often and acted happy to have everyone at home.

My mom, on the other hand, dreaded it when everyone was home at the same time, as inevitably there would be a fight. Sometimes when I was at one of my girlfriends' houses, especially Cheryl's, I had to look up into the ceiling so I could hold back my tears. At times it overwhelmed me to see all the love and fondness they had towards each other. Would Cheryl's parents or sisters notice that I was trying not to cry? What would they think of me? Did they know anything bad about my family? Luckily, I escaped ever having to tell much of anything about myself and became quite expert at avoiding any leading questions.

Eating dinner at my house was the polar opposite from Cheryl's, where everyone gathered at the table, politely passed all the food around, made sure everyone got what they wanted, and seemed more concerned with talking to each other than actually eating. They used the time to catch up on everyone's day. At our house, we didn't have a table. We sat at a counter with stools, sort of like a bar, where we'd all sit in a row, not facing each other. Basically we spent little time talking and concentrated more on eating. The whole dinner was over usually in fifteen or twenty minutes. Everyone ate as fast as they could to get away from the discomfort. The message it sent was hurry, food is to be eaten as quickly as possible, just eat and get the job done. This behavior is toxic for a bulimic as we don't taste food, we simply shove it down our throats as fast as we can, counter to what we learn in recovery.

Mom often complained about how she dreaded cooking dinner. "It's too much work for what little reward you get. There's too much mess to pick up afterwards. It's just too short and not worth all the effort, especially if it's over so soon." Dad always left the table as soon as he was finished and headed straight to the family room to turn on the TV.

I knew I wasn't happy and didn't feel a part of my family, but before going to my friends' houses, I didn't have anything to compare my family with. I was afraid of my dad. I worried if I upset my mom, she would have a nervous break-down. Susan was a stranger to me. Her diving was improving so much she spent every spare minute at the diving school. Carolyn and I were in totally different worlds, but the pain I felt for her at each obstacle she encountered provided a small connection to her.

Being with my friends' families that particular year affected me more so than the one before. Now the contrasts were stark. After being exposed to other fami-lies, I knew I desperately wanted a family that loved each other and wanted to be a part of each others' lives. I yearned for warmth and kindness amongst my par-ents and sisters, but things never moved that way. None of us was thrilled to come to our dreary, unwelcoming home after school or work and spend time with each other. Usually my sisters and I would go to our separate rooms and pass the time until dinner or bed. The only reason to emerge would be to watch one of the big fights that might erupt, which could sometimes last quite a long time and pile on the resulting misery.

I never participated in the fights. Instead, I stood in the background and watched. I didn't have anything to fight about and couldn't understand why everyone else fought, but it didn't matter. I would stand in my bedroom doorway and watch all the running around and screaming and yelling until someone couldn't take it anymore and made the first move to end the chaos.

With the unending turmoil my family created and the increasing amount of trouble that beset us with each passing year, this particular year was, without a doubt, the worst of all. In retrospect, I have to say my mom and dad simply had no clue as to how to deal with us, especially once we were teens and preteen. They met every situation, significant or trivial, with the same reaction: shouting, rage, and resulting despondency. My mom hadn't fully recovered from her MS attack and retreated to her bed daily where she'd lie for hours. She wasn't able to leave the house for any significant amount of time because most buildings had florescent lighting, which she said gave her extreme headaches and made her feel dizzy. She blamed it on her MS. In retrospect, she exhibited all the symptoms of someone with severe depression rather than the MS that has been in remission ever since her initial bout. She was miserable, and it was obvious by her appear-ance. She never bothered to dress up and, overall, looked pale, washed-out, and defeated. She had a sunken, sad look about her face. As for my dad, he was either at work, on a business trip, or mad at everyone except me, usually because I tried very hard to stay out of everyone's way by hiding in my bedroom.

Carolyn was now nearly sixteen, and things hadn't gotten any better from her days in Tiburon. It's hard enough on its own growing up and experiencing teen-

age angst, but looking back now I believe Carolyn's lack of support and the criti-
cism and abuse—verbal and physical—she received must have taken a huge toll
on her and her self-esteem. She made progressively poorer decisions in her life
that many times resulted in her getting into trouble with the law. The nightmares
she put herself through affected not just her but all of us.

One particular night it all finally came to a head, and things for Carolyn and
our family were forever altered. My night started out mundane enough. I was
goofing around in my room, flipping through some magazines and listening to
the soundtrack from "Grease." I loved Olivia Newton John, who I thought was
beautiful, and John Travolta was every girl's dream guy. Susan was in her room
and my mom and dad were in their favorite spots, my mom sitting in the cream
chair in the living room, puffing away at a Carlton cigarette, and my dad sitting
in the family room, watching TV. Somehow we found out Carolyn had run
away. She was gone and didn't want to live with us any longer. I figured Carolyn
finally had enough and wanted to be out of this damned house. As usual, the
shock of the news about her flight was eclipsed by Mom's reaction. All hell broke
loose, and everyone started yelling, panicking, or crying. We all somehow managed to end up in my parent's room. I stood closest to my mom's side of the bed,
Susan stood at the foot, and my dad was by the door, near the hallway.

My mom had to lie down. But as she did, still sobbing uncontrollably, drool
started to drip from the corner of her mouth onto her pillow. Her body shook
violently. She was falling apart. I was devastated. Right in front of my eyes, I saw
her take on the appearance of a helpless child and put aside any semblance of
parental strength. I cried harder than I ever had as I watched her continue to
shake and drool.

Oh, my God, I thought, what's happening to her? I was speechless and even
though my dad and Susan were right there, they didn't do anything. My mom
looked at me, crying, and seemed to simply break down. I was shocked. Nothing
had prepared me for this. I became progressively more distressed. This was the
single worst moment in my life up until then.

Eventually we all had to leave my parents bedroom and, as always, I retreated
to my room, closed my door, and lay on my bed sobbing until there were no
more tears left. The next few days weren't much better. My mom was a wreck
and my dad was enraged. When Carolyn came home finally, I figured everything
would be alright and my Mom would recover.

Things didn't get much better, even after Carolyn returned. She was locked in
a constant battle with my parents. Susan continued to isolate herself as much as
possible by spending all her time at the diving school or dancing at clubs and

discos. I was still too young to be independent, so I was stuck at home, an unwilling witness to the rapid deterioration of the family dynamic. I tried to convince myself to be happy that my mom seemed to get a little better after her breakdown, but she was still emotional and didn't make any effort to hide her feelings from me, which scared me. I was always watching and anticipating that at any moment something terrible would happen to her.

Inevitably, Carolyn ran away from home again and this time when she finally returned, my parents sent her away to live at a halfway house. I didn't fully understand what living in a halfway house meant, but I did understand my parents decided maybe that place could handle her better than they could. But why, if they couldn't help Carolyn, did they yell and scream at her all the time? Surely they must have known how terrible that made her feel. That couldn't help her any. But I never said anything and I'm sure they thought they knew best. I cried in my room all the time she was away. I loved Carolyn and wanted to help her, but I felt powerless and even felt I had failed her. I didn't want her to be sad, but I was so much younger than she was and my mom and dad apparently didn't care about what I felt anyway. I never got over seeing her sent away. I wished my parents could understand how much it hurt to be yelled at, called names, even hit. Then maybe they'd understand why Carolyn was the way she was.

Carolyn's third and final attempt to run away ended with a truly life-altering moment for us all. The events themselves I will not recount here out of respect for my sister but what I will say is that it resulted in my parents isolating us from the outside world. At that age I was unable to understand my parents actions and they neglected ever to explain them to me, instead I withdrew deeper into myself as it seemed did everyone else in the house. During this time we lived an almost shadow-like existence, creeping around in an oppressive silence that was only ever punctured by the screaming fights my parents and Carolyn continued to have.

These events seemed to finally condemn our family to a lifetime of dysfunction, dysfunction that exists today as much as it did back then. Now everyone was hurting and sadness enveloped our house like a toxic cloud. I had no one to help me understand the situation so I thought I should be even quieter and stay out of their way as much as possible. I continued my personal journey inward, retreating from the family, retreating from the world, and seeking solace in the comfort of sugary, sweet food.

This whole situation seemed to take my mother into a darker, more depressed state. She and my father fought more than they ever had in the past. Whatever time I had spent with my mom before faded to almost nothing. Clearly I was the last priority. Carolyn mattered in a negative way. Susan mattered—my dad still devoted his spare time to her, especially her diving—but I was condemned to feed on the leftover scraps of attention. At ten, I felt like yesterday's garbage. My mom would spend time with me only if she was desperate enough and somehow mustered up enough energy. Otherwise, I was on my own.

This didn't bring my dad and me any closer. It did nothing. I didn't know him before, and I didn't know him any better now. Susan didn't want to be with me either. So, I decided I better be a very good girl, do nothing wrong, and not say anything to anyone. My mom couldn't afford to be any more upset or my dad any angrier. I would have to try and make sense of everything and everyone by myself. I wasn't managing very well. I usually cried, which was all my mixed-up emotional being could do.

Chapter 6

From a Whisper to a Silent Scream

Even today I believe all the emotional traumas people experience throughout their childhood years defines significantly who we are as adults and affects the way we live our lives. At age ten, my lack of self-worth and self-esteem began to overwhelm me and ultimately paved the way for my choosing food and bulimia as my answer to everything.

In my head, I pictured a perfect family. But that family was make-believe and in no way resembled mine. On the contrary, they were all fighting to survive in their own, separate world. I decided I had no other choice but to empower myself to create another world outside my actual one, and I began to do so. I decided this secret place would be where I could go to seek some level of comfort I needed but wasn't receiving elsewhere. I turned my feelings inward rather than trying to find answers from the outside. I thought I could deal with all my confused emotions more easily this way and have some control. I had the ability to make believe if I needed to and often I would do just that. I'd make believe everything was fine in my home and that all this stuff going on was normal. Somehow by turning my emotions inward and not expressing them, I intertwined them with feelings of inadequacy about myself. If I couldn't control what was going on in my outside world and if I couldn't express my true feelings, then I would find something I could control and gain some sense of grounding. I began to focus more of my time and energy on what I felt was wrong with me than what was wrong with my family life. I couldn't change my mom, dad, or sisters but I did know I had the ability to change myself. I hyper-focused on every negative characteristic I imagined existed about myself and pondered how I could change them.

By now my insecurities about my outer appearance had increased and I spent a lot of time day dreaming about how I could change the way I looked. If I did find a way to change my appearance, I thought, then maybe my family would care about me. I came up with no real solutions. Instead, any time I felt confused, sad, depressed, or just lonely I'd go to my room, close my door, and cry until I could cry no more. I was becoming better and better and was mastering my craft of soothing myself through crying and burying my feelings rather than expressing them and ridding myself of them. But crying wasn't enough sometimes. I was becoming more dependant on food and the comfort and love I felt it provided me. I knew I was getting bigger by eating, but I couldn't find any other useful tool to calm me down and make me feel some level of reassurance. I was becoming codependent on the false pleasures food brought for me.

I convinced my mom, through sheer persistence, to let me attend sixth grade at a public junior high school rather than St. Isidore's where I disliked the nuns and never felt like I belonged. My transition to junior high was the perfect time to transfer to another school. It didn't hurt my argument that Stone Valley Junior High was within walking distance of our house, relieving my mom of having to take me to and from school every day. Monica wanted to leave St. Isidore's, too, and she convinced her parents to let her transfer to Stone Valley, a major coup and cause for celebration for the two of us. I was looking forward to going to a non-Catholic school. I could wear regular clothes, and I wouldn't have nuns for teachers. The pressure to be good while trying to fit in wasn't proving to be successful for me. I knew this was my chance to try and reinvent myself.

School began and although Monica and I were not in any classes together, we hung out during the breaks. I immediately liked Stone Valley and knew going there was the right decision. There were many more kids I could become friends with, and I felt like I had more freedom overall. Just being able to create my own identity through wearing clothes I liked, rather than an ugly school jumper, made me feel more comfortable too. I thought I might be able to camouflage my growing body parts, particularly my stomach and butt, and at the same time try to fit in with my classmates by choosing outfits like theirs.

The events of the previous months changed Carolyn forever. She was now so quiet, it would have been impossible not to notice how depressed she was. We could hear her endless sobbing when we walked by her bedroom. There was another dimension of sadness to her now, not just related to the misery surrounding her relationship with my parents. She completely altered her lifestyle. She no longer hung out with the stoner crowd and started helping the handicapped. She threw herself headlong into religion and conservative thinking, a path she follows to this day.

Susan was more involved in her social life than ever, hanging out at discos with her friends. As time went by, I saw less and less of her.

Both my parents went back to their patterned lifestyles. My mom continued to feel sick all the time and retreated to her bedroom to lie down for hours each day or sit in her favorite chair, puffing away on her cigarettes. My dad continued to work non-stop. The fighting and yelling weren't taking place as often, but the gloom that hung over the place was ever present.

In September I was excited about becoming a seventh grader. This year I wouldn't be in the class at the bottom of the totem pole. I was in the middle and with that came a level of seniority. I had made some new friends the previous year and Monica and I had remained friends, although we weren't nearly as close as we had been back at St. Isidore's.

Aside from school, what dominated my thoughts now was my rapid increase in body fat. I had slowly become aware that I used food not just to fill my empty stomach. It seemed the more depressed or anxious I got, the more I clung to food. I somehow lost that the purpose of food was to nourish my body and looked to it to nourish my hungry heart. The more I ate, the worse I felt about myself, but I couldn't control my comfort eating. All my friends would eat junk food, candy, ice-cream, and cookies, and I would willingly join in. I wanted to be like them. But even when I ate with them, I wasn't satisfied and would look for any opportunity to sneak more food.

By the time eighth grade began, I was hanging out with a group of girls and guys. I looked forward to spending time with those I hadn't seen over summer break. Despite the fact I had gained a lot of weight over the past school year and summer—partly because I didn't swim on the team, I was too embarrassed to wear a bathing suit in front of my teammates—I wasn't prepared for the reaction of my friends and family. I now tipped the scale at close to one hundred fifty-five pounds, but the reality of weighing that much hadn't sunk in. I was only five-three and when my mom and I went to Emporium Capwell's in Walnut Creek for some new school clothes, to my embarrassment I needed to try on twelves and fourteens.

She didn't say too much in the fitting room, but I could tell by the look of horror on her face that she was upset at my size. She stood there staring at my undressed body with its fat rolls and cellulite covering nearly every inch. I tried not to notice her glare and look of disapproval as I proceeded to try on the school clothes I had chosen. I didn't want to face the fact that I was truly fat and that I had some strange problem with food. As I looked at my backside in the dressing room mirror, I couldn't deny the fact that my butt was huge, but I struggled to remain focused on how excited I was about being in the eighth grade. I tried on numerous tops and slacks. After a long and painful afternoon, I finally found several outfits.

When we got home, I went to my room, trying to put aside the indignities of the day and my mom's disapproving looks. I tried on all my new clothes again, studying myself in the mirror with each combination. I wanted to wear my best outfit the first day.

I walked to school with my neighbor, Karen, happy with my new baby-blue corduroy pants, white top, and my knock-off Cherokee sandals. I got to school extra early so I could spend time talking with my friends before classes started. The joyful reunion I had anticipated turned into something else. What I had denied all summer long, especially during my shopping outing with my mom, hit me square between the eyes. I realized I was fat. None of my friends wore near the size I did. It didn't matter that I had no clue what size they actually did wear, because I could tell by their overall appearance they were much slimmer than I was. Some of their faces, particularly the ones I hadn't seen over the summer, registered surprise at my appearance. Instantly, I realized I hadn't been able to hide my big, fat body in the lovely new clothes. But rather than thinking what I could do to lose weight, I wanted to eat anything I could get my hands on right then and there. When classes began, I walked to my homeroom and drifted into space as the teacher went over the year's lessons.

I reflected on my day as I dragged myself home. Although my mom had spent several hundred dollars on new clothes for me, they now seemed ugly and meaningless. I was too fat and my friends thought I was fat. Their unspoken comments provoked a strange new set of feelings within me, a combination of anxiety and sadness that would dominate my thinking for the next two decades.

Everything seemed to be deteriorating for me. There was no change at home, and now school was worse than before. I felt like I had just gone through an entire day of being battered, only there were no visible marks on my body, just open wounds on my heart. That evening I tried on all my new clothes again, hoping that one of the outfits would make me look less fat so I could wear that the next day and erase today. No matter which ones I tried on, I looked the same. With the images of family and friends turning their faces away from my grotesque form spinning in my head, I turned to my worst enemy and my new best friend, food. My need to taste something pleasing to experience some level of comfort was becoming an addiction I couldn't control. The more negative my feelings, the more food I ate.

Several weeks had passed and my feelings about my self worth were diminishing day by day. I felt devalued as a person and believed that the only thing that mattered to anyone I knew was how I looked on the outside. My silent cries for help remained, as always, unanswered, ignored. My mom didn't seem to notice the sadness I felt or the long hours spent crying alone in my bedroom. I wished for a miracle to reverse the cycle but instead, I just ate and ate, which inevitably lead to packing on more weight.

I thought I'd hit the lowest point in my life the morning I stumbled out the front door after gorging on a huge breakfast, complete with bowls of cereal, slices of toast, sweet rolls, and orange juice. I couldn't face another day at school feeling this way. I bent over in the bushes in front of my house, placed three fingers down my throat, and gagged until all the food I had just devoured came up. I felt like I was two people: the one who lived deep inside me unable to express her feelings, and the one who told me to get rid of all that bad food I had just stuffed into my big fat face. If I somehow got rid of it, then and only then, would the real me feel better. Amazingly it worked. I did feel better. I felt much less anxious and more importantly, I didn't feel as fat as I had just minutes ago. Would this euphoric feeling last? I didn't know. I only knew I couldn't stand feeling fat and disgusting for another minute and if this act helped alleviate that, then at least I could be momentarily euphoric. The inner voice that told me to put my fingers down my throat and expel all the toxic food I'd just eaten spoke the first comforting words I'd heard in a very long time.

Immediately afterwards, as I looked at the breakfast that lay on the ground before me, I had no choice but to pull myself together, as there were only minutes to spare before my neighbor, Karen, would appear so we could walk to school together. Not fully realizing what I'd just experienced, I decided that for now I'd have to focus my attention on talking with Karen and then going to my classes.

The intensity of the experience prevented me from dismissing it and through the entire day, I couldn't concentrate either in class or even at break. I was physically present, but my mind was racing with questions. "Did I find a cure to my fatness?" "Did I discover how I can eat and at the same time not gain weight?"

I had so many questions. I was desperate to feel like I was important and I was willing to do anything to achieve it. Throwing up seemed like an easy solution. I didn't know anyone who did this, and I wasn't entirely sure how I came up with the idea. It didn't matter. I cared only that I no longer felt like I was going to explode and be even more unworthy of being liked. Whether I would make myself throw up again or not, I had no idea. But at that moment, I felt calmer and didn't worry about weighing more when I got on the scale later that day.

I hated myself so much I had to find a way to release my feelings and numb my pain. If no one was going to provide comfort to me then I had to give it to myself. Food became my sole source of self-comfort. I was addicted to the feelings it gave me such as the momentary rush of joy when a cold spoonful of ice-cream melted in my mouth or when I'd eat a huge bowl of cereal and savor that crunching sensation.

Although I sought comfort in food, at the same time I was aware that it caused me to gain weight, which ultimately made me feel worse about myself. I had to come up with a way to control my food, otherwise, I knew I would one day wake up obese and unable to ever lose the weight. I decided that night something had provided me with the solution and from then on I would throw up whatever I ate and prevent my spiral into obesity. As those days and weeks went by, I slowly accepted that this was what I had to do and this was how I had to live my life. Eat and eat for comfort and pleasure and then throw it all up. Simple.

I developed a love-hate relationship with food. I realized my bulimic lifestyle was dictating every action. After that first morning when I threw up in the bushes, I was forever changed. I began to binge and purge nearly every day. Soon I found myself consuming more and more food as the months passed. Often I would eat two or even three thousand calories per binge and purge episode. At first I would binge and purge only before school but after several weeks, I began to do it after school as well.

Chapter 7

Unseen in Plain Sight

From the time my mom married my dad, she had not worked outside the home. Now that I was throwing up all the time, I wished she did work so she wasn't around so much. I always felt that she wasn't a typical stay-at-home mom anyway. She never participated in any of my school activities, including open house. She never joined the PTA, volunteered for any school events, or even took my friends and me out for a bicycle ride or to see a movie. My mom was always at home, but the majority of the time, she was either in bed or sitting in her chair, lost in her own thoughts.

My two sisters were now adults. Carolyn, well over her troubled youth, had become an extreme, conservative Catholic. Susan was at college and working very aggressively to make money. Apparently my mom decided she would focus her energies and woes on me. I began to hate the fact that now she wanted to know everything I was doing or where I was going, not in a good way, but in a controlling manner designed to provide opportunities for her to disapprove, scold, or pass judgment. If I didn't tell her everything, she'd snoop in my personal belongings or listen to my phone conversations. This transition from never talking to me or noticing me to monitoring my every move was oppressive and confusing. How was it she could still ignore my feelings and obvious sadness, but wanted to know who I was talking to and what I was doing in the kitchen?

What distressed me far beyond her nagging was her constant harassment about what I was eating. She had decided at some point I was not the correct size or shape and began a constant barrage of comments about my weight and appearance. She had always asked about my day, but this year and the years to follow, her comments were far more destructive. I had become overweight roughly the same time my two sisters began the different chapters in their lives. My mom had no one, no relationship with my dad, no friends, no activities, no hobbies, so she fixated on my appearance and made that the center of her life, her mission.

She constantly nagged and tried to convince me that the only way I'd be happy was to lose weight and be skinny. She prided herself on having an eighteen-inch waist on her wedding day and continued to take pride in her very slim figure. To me she seemed to only care about how I looked and not who I was. This was terribly upsetting and confusing. I couldn't understand why she never did anything with me, for me, or for herself, other than focus on the weight issue. It was no secret I was fat, but didn't my mom know that her disapproving comments prompted horrible feelings in me? Basically, her words and actions simply translated as "quit eating and lose weight or I will not be able to accept you for who you are." To this day, I can hear her shouting, "Jocelyn, what are you eating?" "Jocelyn, you better stop eating now. You've been in the kitchen long enough." And the worst, "Jocelyn, if you'd only lose weight everything would be fine."

I'd cringe when I'd hear her utter those ugly words from the living room where, like clockwork, she'd always be after I arrived home from school. I felt like she was both the judge and jury, sitting there puffing away at her cigarettes, yelling at me to quit eating, and deciding whether I was fit to be accepted in her version of society. She never let up and her remarks succeeded only in making me feel even more insecure, unworthy, and, ultimately, frantic.

I couldn't escape from myself and my weight no matter where I was, not at school and not at home. Instead of trying to support me, my mom's words and facial expressions continued to confirm that I was nothing more than a worthless fat person, which compelled me do the opposite of what she wanted. I would eat even more food, to the point where it was impossible to eat another morsel. Then I would feel so guilty I had to punish myself for being fat and gorging. In my mind, that left no other choice but to throw up everything I had just stuffed my face with. Her remarks would never create a miracle, make me change, and suddenly lose weight. Her constant nagging didn't bring about an epiphany, awakening me fully inspired with renewed energy to lose weight. Ultimately, her remarks hurt me more than those of my classmates. I felt even my own mother didn't like me for who I was.

I spiraled down a path of further introversion where food became even more important to me. My binges were increasing and becoming more frequent. My deep, painful feelings of sadness and despair increased. I felt I wasn't wanted anywhere.

As I continued to binge and purge daily, I became desperate for a way to control my food addiction. I tried to convince myself to simply not eat, but that didn't work. Since I'd been raised a Catholic, in a strict Catholic home, I started to pray, not just during Sunday mass, but everyday in my bedroom. My addiction to prayer took full force in just a couple weeks. At first I would recite the usual Catholic prayers, a couple Our Fathers and Hail Mary's. But I felt those prayers were not being heard. I decided I'd have to increase my volume of prayers and the length of time I devoted to praying. It got to the point that I felt like I was unable to start my day if I did not spend a certain amount of time praying.

The situation was further confused by the fact I already believed I was somewhat doomed to hell because my mother's representation of the faith made it a catch-22. Whatever I did ended up being a sin of some sort. She would often lecture me about sex, not anything in detail, just that it was a mortal sin and I would go to hell if I did those bad acts or even if I just thought about them. According to the faith, thinking about doing something was just as bad as doing it. Her mission and duty was to instill the fear of God in me, just as her mother had done to her. "Jocelyn, sex is a mortal sin." "Jocelyn, doing anything bad is a sin." "Jocelyn you don't want to go to hell, do you?" Funny, I could always watch a violent TV show or movie, but anything that had sex in it was forbidden.

I thought about doing things with boys, I used God's name in vain, I told the occasional lie, and I even drank alcohol. Not long after I started eighth grade, I began drinking on the weekends with my friends. We'd all steal booze from our parents. My mom drank vodka, so it was easy for me to steal it. I'd just replace whatever I took with water. She never noticed. To try and reconcile my "double life" of good little Catholic and rampaging sinner, I felt I could save my soul only through constant prayer. I committed to a morning ritual in the belief it would help God forgive my sins and consider me a candidate for heaven. Even more so, I wanted God to hear my pleas and help me overcome my horrible addiction to food. Everyday when I woke up, I'd turn on the light beside my bed and get my numerous prayers out of my top dresser drawer. Then I would begin to recite Novenas—prayers that are supposed to have the power of answering whatever it is you ask of God if you recite them properly—for at least forty minutes. Only then did I feel I had devoted enough time and, possibly, God would hear me.

Not long after I began compulsively praying, I realized no one was listening—not God, not the Saints, not even the angels. I felt utterly hopeless and more depressed than ever. I contemplated committing suicide. How would I do it? Should I cut my wrists? I could do that in the bathroom. Nobody would bother me until it was already too late. Should I take a bottle of aspirin and down it with alcohol? That might be better. I would keep that one in the back of my mind, as that seemed like a good choice. Or should I just take one of my dad's many guns and shoot myself in the head? I couldn't decide which one was best. God, I am so messed up. Why aren't you hearing my prayers? What aren't you taking away all my pain? Why aren't you helping me to stop throwing up?

I felt undeserving of God's love. My mom had convinced me I was a terrible sinner. Sunday mass sermons reinforced this. And now I was convinced God thought the same because of my unanswered prayers, but still I continued my daily routine. I'd wake up, pray for forty minutes, take a shower, and finish getting ready for school, and then go to the kitchen to begin my day of binging and purging. After, I'd go to school and pretend everything was fine, hiding my insecurities as best as I could.

I tried to conceal the total pain I was in and the feeling that suicide was my only option. I'm thankful I never did follow through with any of my suicide ideas but the thoughts stayed with me for many years to come. I knew, according to the Catholic Church, if I committed suicide, I'd be damned to go straight to hell. Fearful of that, I thought I'd wait a while in the hope things would change.

Through all that, my mother was either in her room lying on her bed or in the living room in the cream-colored chair beside the fireplace. She'd sit there for hours and hours, smoking cigarette after cigarette, just staring into space. That's how I saw it.

If my mom was in her chair when I got home from school, I'd enter the kitchen as quietly as possible. Then I'd shove as much food into me as I was able because after about ten minutes she would come into the kitchen and scrutinize what I was eating. Prior to that, she'd shout from her chair, "What are you eating? Haven't you had enough? You need to watch your weight. You won't be able to eat your dinner if you keep on eating."

I'd try to block out her remarks and continue to gorge on anything I could easily scarf down that required little to no preparation, things like bread, cereal, cookies, and crackers. If I was feeling especially daring, I'd pop a frozen dinner into the microwave. I was like a machine on auto-pilot, dumping garbage into a bottomless pit. Eating became almost mechanical because the faster I ate, the more I could shove down my throat, and the less I actually tasted. When I reached the point I thought I should stop because I was running out of private time and didn't want to get caught with my mouth and hands full, I'd casually go straight to the bathroom.

Occasionally my mom asked why I was going into the bathroom. Naturally she had suspicions about my behaviors, but she never acted on them. I'd tell her either my stomach hurt or that I was going to take a bath.

Everything I did in terms of binging and purging had some sort of process. Once in the bathroom, I'd decide on the best way to disguise what I was about to do. That meant trying to cover up any possible noises I might make. If I said I was taking a bath, this bought me the time I needed to complete a purge session and recuperate before emerging. The noise from the running and draining water would mute any sounds I made throwing up. I couldn't focus on anything but trying to get rid of all the "bad" food I'd just eaten. Not even my mom's cruel remarks could change me and make me stop eating huge quantities of food. I tuned her out as much as possible, with the aid of the sensations food provided.

Both my parents were very appearance conscious. Their reactions and actions towards me strengthened my awareness that my image and self-worth were tied to how I looked and contributed to my leading a double life. To others, I was Jocelyn, the plump little thirteen-year-old who was just trying to fit in and be liked, while at the same time I was Jocelyn, the depressed and lonely thirteen-year-old who felt she wasn't a valuable person, who could only feel comfort or acceptance through food.

I suppose the seeds for my eating disorder were planted when I was much younger, but my experiences and the remarks I received left deep scars that prompted its hardcore manifestation. Food filled the void left by the absence of the love and appreciation I desperately wanted.

PART II
THE BETRAYAL

Chapter 8

My Demon Makes Its Home

My secret life of binging and purging continued, and I began an endless cycle of costly weight loss programs. By early winter my weight had reached an all-time high and no matter how much I ate and threw up or how little I'd try to eat if I wasn't going to throw it up, I still remained fat and emotionally lost.

Within a month or so after the start of eighth grade, my mother tried to convince me that if I lost weight I would become a petite teen and everything would just fall into its proper place. She was relentless in harassing me about it. How could she possibly think I didn't know I was fat? Did she think I needed her to remind me in case I'd somehow forgotten? I wasn't losing weight no matter what I tried. In exasperation, my mom decided it would be best if I went to a weight loss facility and followed their regimen for losing my unwanted fat.

In October I embarked on my first paid-for weight loss program, Diet Center. It was a well-known diet facility. My older sister, Susan, had participated in their program. She never had a weight issue and, in all honesty, I don't know why she went.

I went to the small building in the back streets of Danville, behind Burger King, where a little old lady told my mom and me about the program. She went over the foods they allowed clients to eat, exactly how much they were allowed to have, and suggested to my mother that she buy one of the small food scales at the supermarket so I wouldn't go over my allowed portions. After she went over the program and foods, I followed her into the back room where I'd face my worst enemy, the scale. One step after the other, I got on the huge scale and watched in despair as she moved the weight more and more to the right. Finally she stopped at one hundred sixty-four pounds.

I wanted to die right then and there. Now my mom knew how much I weighed and worse, now I knew how much I weighed. I couldn't pretend to myself any longer. I couldn't try to camouflage my rolls of fat by wearing baggy clothes. I was standing on the scale staring at the huge number displayed in front of me. My mom was standing right beside me while the lady wrote it down on my chart, which she would keep to record my progress. I was mortified and numb with humiliation. We followed her to a room that looked like a small grocery store consisting of prepackaged food made exclusively for Diet Center clients.

We bought a week's supply of dehydrated food and little pills, supplements whose ingredients are a mystery to me to this day. When we finished, my grocery bag consisted of a less-than-mouthwatering collection of powdered cereals, pancake mix, little packets of salad dressing, and what I soon discovered were extremely tasteless little crackers.

Once we left that horrible place, my mom drove directly to the grocery store to buy me the rest of the diet food I needed. I had sat in the corner the entire time, listening to the little old lady talk about how I was going to lose lots of weight and get thin, but I could only think about how ugly and disgusting I felt. Everyone now knew how fat I was, and there would be no avoiding the pressure my mom would exert. I hoped this diet would be the answer to my problems, that I would lose weight and finally be important to someone. But in the back of my mind, I knew I had far bigger problems than just worrying about boiling some water and adding it to the little tiny package of Diet Center powder. I knew I couldn't control myself for very long and felt certain I wouldn't be able to stay on this diet long enough to lose all the weight I needed to lose.

When we returned home, I trudged to the kitchen to unpack my food for the week. Once the groceries were unloaded, I walked straight to my room where I could be alone and cry. To add to my humiliation, it didn't take long for my friends at school to find out I was on a diet. Every lunch hour I'd bring my little brown paper bag to the cafeteria where one by one I'd take out all the tasteless foods, trying my best to play it down in front of my friends. Naturally they noticed. I told them my mom took me to Diet Center to lose weight. I could tell by the looks on their faces they agreed with my mom about my need to lose weight. Each day I'd eat the dry, tasteless food for lunch and to my surprise, I began losing weight. The very next week at my weigh-in, I'd lost four and a half pounds. I felt good that I could get on the scary scale and have the Diet Center lady move it down to the left a little rather than up to the right.

The weight loss motivated me to continue the program and see if I could lose even more. I was able to avoid binging that first week because I targeted all my energy into losing weight and following the program. But what surprised me even more than my ability to go without throwing up was my sudden obsession with losing weight. From the very start of the program, I no longer wanted to accept the label of fat kid or even the fat kid who had to pay for a diet to lose weight.

I hated myself and hated going each week to the building behind Burger King to get weighed in front of my diet leader and my mom, but I lasted an entire month before I caved in emotionally and physically and binged and purged. I couldn't take eating all the crappy food, let alone feeling humiliated day after day. "Jocelyn is so fat, she has to go on a diet." The pressure to lose weight was overwhelming for me. I didn't throw up just one time. I threw up over and over, for a week straight. By the time I stepped on the scale at Diet Center again, the diet leader moved the weight to the right. I had gained three and a half pounds.

I was embarrassed and lied to my mom and my diet leader. I pretended to be just as baffled as they were and said I didn't know how I could have gained weight. When my mom and I drove home, I could tell she was very disappointed in me. She had thought this program was going to make me thin and accepted by others. She always excluded herself in this, but who was she kidding? She didn't accept me as a fat kid. I had to become thin for her just as much as for anyone else.

I lied as best I could and told her this week would be different. It sure was. I didn't stop binging and purging. I also started sneaking food that wasn't on my diet. My mom caught me a few times eating foods I wasn't supposed to have. She simply stared at me with disdain and reminded me I wasn't supposed to be eating this or that. I didn't know how to properly handle all the pressure I was feeling. I didn't know how to communicate my feelings. Worse than that, I knew if I tried to talk to my mom, she wouldn't want to hear what I was saying.

Another week passed and I lost no weight. I told my mom I just couldn't continue doing the Diet Center program. I needed a break. She let me quit, but I knew she wasn't at all happy with my decision. In her eyes, I was still the fat thirteen-year-old.

It was quite obvious to me I wasn't considered a valuable person in my current state. I figured the only way to avoid the rude remarks I received at home and at school was to continue my weight loss quest without the aid of Diet Center. I used what calorie and portion control knowledge I had acquired and focused all my energy into fully understanding the caloric amounts in the food I was eating. I began to count my calories religiously, knowing I had to cut back to achieve my goal. I was more determined than ever to succeed and be recognized as a person. By focusing all my inner energy on finding ways to lose weight, I was able to stop binging and purging during this time.

Two weeks after quitting the program, I started restricting my caloric intake. At first I tried to eat about twelve hundred calories a day with very similar foods to that of Diet Center—fruits, vegetables, eggs, chicken, and Wasa crackers. I did begin to lose weight. My clothes were becoming looser, and I was feeling more empowered to continue this new journey. I believed I could handle eating fewer calories than twelve hundred and decided to limit myself to between eight hundred fifty and nine hundred calories a day. The weight was coming off and now even my classmates and my mom told me I was starting to look good, that they could tell I was losing weight.

These new feelings I started having as a result of the feedback from my mom and friends confirmed my thoughts about myself. *I will be more important and accepted if I continue my journey to lose weight.* Soon my compulsion to binge and purge took another form, restricting. Again not satisfied with the amount of calories I was eating, I made the commitment to myself to eat even less, just four hundred fifty calories a day. Day by day I was becoming more and more fixated on what foods I would allow myself and how much weight I was losing. Instead of feeling numb through bulimia, I was able to feel numb through restricting. I found being in a constant state of numbness easier than riding my emotional roller coaster of negative feelings.

Choosing not to eat worked and I lost about fifty-eight pounds. I now weighed one hundred six. I was thrilled I'd lost so much and had found a way to succeed in doing so. But deep inside, I knew I'd basically starved myself. I wasn't aware I might be harming myself because I only cared about becoming thin.

I was completely obsessed with not eating now and it seemed to be less time-consuming and less taxing on my body than throwing up. For once I felt like I fitted in with my classmates. I went from a size fourteen to a size three in just a couple months. My family started to take more interest in me—not much, but at least my mother stopped commenting on my need to lose weight and my classmates were also friendlier to me. It was clear everyone acted differently around the thin me than the fat me. I had boys pursuing me and girls wanting to be my friend. I felt like a new person, as if I finally achieved some level of respect with my mom and the rest of my family to some degree and my classmates.

The biggest surprise for me was that still, somehow, I didn't feel any different on the inside than I did when I weighed one hundred sixty-four. I still felt fat and unworthy. Maybe even more unworthy because rather than feeling joy at receiving all this new attention, I knew I was only receiving it because I had lost so much weight. It could all evaporate in an instant of weight gain. No one saw me for me. My personality hadn't changed. My likes and dislikes hadn't changed.

But because I had worked so hard to lose weight, I tried to ignore those nagging feelings. I knew I wasn't respected as a person when I was fat and having at least some attention paid to me now was preferable to having none.

I was so thrilled with taking off almost sixty pounds in just a few months that I never thought what I was doing might be unhealthy. I thought only of how wonderful losing weight was. My mother thought nothing of the fact I'd dropped so much weight in such a short time. The only feedback I received from her and anyone else was positive. "Jocelyn, you look so good now that you have lost weight." "Jocelyn, you're so little now." And from my mom, who had bought me several new outfits as a reward. "Jocelyn, how nice you look in your new clothes."

Unfortunately, as successful as I thought my new way of eating and losing weight was, it did not come without consequences. My body collapsed, and I was diagnosed with mononucleosis. The lack of proper nutritional balance had depleted essential vitamins and minerals. I simply couldn't take the strain I had placed on myself any longer. In my heart, I knew I had gotten mono because I was so tired and weak from trying to eat almost nothing, just to please others.

I wanted my mom to tell me my rapid weight loss wasn't good. I was hoping she'd notice my erratic behavior, but she did not. The doctor knew nothing of my radical weight loss, so after our visit was finished we went home where I once again went to my room. I was too sick now to muster up even the slightest bit of energy, and the doctor said that because my mono was so severe, I would be out of school for a couple months. I needed to rest, regain my strength, and get myself feeling better.

I couldn't believe it. I always thought mono was the kissing disease, that girls got it by kissing a boy who had it. I was mistaken. My extreme eating habits had just broken my body. My mom hadn't cared how I lost the weight, only that I had. She was unconcerned about the methods I'd used to accomplish it. I was both angry and sad about the fact that the result was all that mattered and my health meant so little. Besides, I knew now what mattered to her, the rest of my family, and my classmates—I was no longer fat, I was skinny.

For the next two months I stayed home unable to attend school. I was too weak the majority of the time to care about missing out on any gossip or fun activities. I certainly wasn't focused on my scholastics, even though I maintained good grades, so that element never bothered me. I felt so beaten up by now that in some ways I welcomed the rest.

Once I was feeling better, my appetite naturally started to increase. I wasn't willing to go back to eating everything in sight, especially because I had worked so hard to lose weight. But I was willing to eat just a little more than I allowed myself prior to coming down with mono.

I counted calories, very careful at first to watch what I was eating. I started out by allowing myself up to eight hundred calories a day. My first day of post-mono eating I indulged myself with a lean serving of cube steak and some peas for dinner in addition to my usual diet of apples and yogurt. I hadn't had any type of protein in months and was looking forward to eating a small piece of steak. To my horror, the following morning I gained a pound. I was devastated. What was going on? I had eaten eight hundred calories before and hadn't gained weight.

I tried to relax and blame it on water weight. Maybe cube steak had a lot of sodium in it, and I hadn't calculated that. I tried the next day to remain positive and keep on track with eating eight hundred calories a day. Same kinds of foods I had been eating during my stint with Diet Center and my own diet, but again the scale said I had gained weight. I was now up a pound and a half. I didn't understand. I was so hungry all day long. How could I be gaining weight? I worked hard to lose all the fat and now it seemed like I no longer had control over my body. I was starting to doubt myself. I was starting to think about having a huge binge and purge session. I needed something and food was what I used in the past to feel something or, more accurately, not to feel anything.

The next day I again gained weight, only this time I decided to give in to my impulses. Racing into the kitchen in the early hours of the morning, I grabbed everything I could get my hands on: bread and butter, cereal, pastries, orange juice, even cheese and crackers. I was on a mission to eat as much as I could in as little time as possible. No one was up yet except my dad, who was already gone. He was at the coffee shop down the road where he went religiously every morning, Monday through Sunday, to eat eggs and toast and talk with the locals. I had complete privacy. As quietly as possible, I managed to stuff myself to the point of nearly fainting before I went into the bathroom just down the hall from the kitchen to throw up everything. I was frantic during this whole ordeal, but I also knew that despite feeling anxious and depressed, once I finished throwing up I would be too weak and numb to care, at least for a while.

Later that day as I sat in my algebra class, I couldn't focus on anything Mr. Herbert was teaching. My mind wandered into another place, and I thought about how discouraged I was. I had worked so hard to lose weight and make myself feel valued. Now I felt like I hadn't accomplished anything. My hopes and dreams shattered. I couldn't fight this battle any longer. I had caved in and knew this bulimic episode would be one of many to come.

Within a period of three months, I regained all but twelve pounds of the weight I had taken off. I now weighed one hundred fifty-two pounds. This time my body grew in places it hadn't before, redistributing my fat differently. My butt grew larger than it ever had been and my stomach and back carried so much extra fat that anyone could see the rolls from every angle. For a brief while I was a size three. Now I was a size twelve, and I felt awful about myself.

The kids at school began to look at me differently again. I could feel the stares behind my back. Monica was especially mean to me. Right to my face, she looked me up and down and shook her head in disgust. Had she no idea how horrible I felt about myself? Had she no idea how much her nasty and very obvious mocking looks hurt me? Didn't Monica care about the fact that we had been such good friends? I guessed not. It seemed to be in Monica's nature to be drawn to slim people as she herself had a slim figure and her new best friend did too. To add fuel to my blazing fire of guilt, my old boyfriend, who I went out with throughout seventh grade, announced to all our friends that I was now too fat to be his girlfriend again.

My face turned bright red as everyone stared at me in the middle of the school corridor. After he said those painful words to me, I ran into the bathroom and started to cry. I couldn't hold my tears back as I stood in the stall with the door locked. I was able to hold in my tears when Monica or anyone else ridiculed me as I passed by, but I wasn't able to do so when Kurt did it in front of so many people. Eventually Monica came and made a token gesture at consoling me. But Kurt's cruel words had cut into me and made me much warier of boys in general from that point forward.

Because my flirtation with being thin was so brief, I never shed the fat girl image. I felt like a failure. I relied more and more on the comfort of food and the numbness bulimia brought me. When eighth grade graduation arrived, I was binging and purging morning and night.

Chapter 9

Diet Slave

I was now completely and utterly addicted to my bulimia. Throwing up was no longer a choice for me, it was a necessity, like breathing. Bulimia was my panacea for everything. If I was sad I binged, if I was happy I binged. I had no other tools to use to cope with my life other than my bulimic rituals. I felt desperate and hopeless, alone with my disease, the demon who was my one constant companion.

I dreaded going to my new high school, Monte Vista, which was located just minutes up the road from my house and where I'd spend the next four years of my life. Before attending Monte Vista, I knew it was well known around town and the surrounding towns, for being very rich, snotty, and competitive. I wasn't cute or thin, and I knew I'd never be popular. I was in for a long hard ride. It was impossible for me to compete with the wealth, good looks, and money most of the kids had. The primary feeders for the students attending Monte Vista were affluent residential communities. Not only did I lack the wealth of most of the students, but I also lacked confidence. I wouldn't be able to overcome the image I had. I felt sick just thinking about going to Monte Vista High School.

During the summer, I tried several homemade diets, but to no avail. Rather, I seemed to binge and purge more so than during the school year. I would start my freshman year at Monte Vista fat, just like I was while attending Stone Valley. I felt like a failure.

The first day of school I tried to pretend I was just as excited to be in high school as all my friends were. I managed to put on a brave front and face the music. I don't know what possessed me to wear a big burgundy and white stripped rugby shirt that day, but as soon as I got to campus, I regretted my choice tenfold. Everyone was more dressed up than I had ever seen at school. I felt out of place with my big stomach, big boobs, and huge shoulders. I looked more like I was ready to try out for the football team. As I headed to my first class of the day, I couldn't stop myself from walking through the halls with my head tilted, eyes downcast. I didn't want to be noticed and certainly didn't want to make eye contact with any of the seniors.

I was very grateful that I'd finally made another best friend back in eighth grade, but I also knew I couldn't reveal my true self or my worries to her. If my mom couldn't handle them, surely Stacy couldn't. I wasn't about to take the chance of losing the only real friend I had. I cared for her and valued our friendship, but even the security of having a best friend didn't ease the pressure I felt.

Everywhere I looked, I saw hundreds of thin, attractive people. Alamo is one of the most affluent communities in all of California, and it's filled with many beautiful people. Being surrounded by them simply increased my anxiety and insecurity.

My home life provided no meaningful support or help in developing interpersonal skills. Meanwhile, most of the girls I knew seemed to develop into well-rounded people during high school, where their confidence, self-worth, and self-esteem grew. On the contrary, my high school years further fueled my negative self-image. I lapsed deeper into my depression and deeper into being bulimic.

Every weekday was the same. My alarm woke me from a restless sleep each morning at six. I'd shower and get ready for school. Once my beauty routine was completed, I headed straight to the kitchen, knowing I would eat whatever I could and throw it all up before seven thirty. My routine had changed little from the previous year except that my stomach could hold more food. I was obsessed with the same binge foods—cereal, bread, and sugary provisions. I loved carbohydrates and could never seem to get enough of them. I could now complete my entire bulimic ritual in twenty-five minutes, start to finish. But this year, I was eating more, around four thousand calories, just for my morning binge.

I couldn't get away with binging and purging at school. I never felt comfortable eating in front of people let alone stuffing my face in front of them, especially now that I was in high school, so I'd eat a small package of pretzels and two Fig Newtons for lunch everyday. I still counted calories, even if I purged. I estimated my lunch totaled around five hundred calories and that seemed reasonable to me if I wasn't going to throw up.

I'd watch while my classmates ate everything from hamburgers with chips to candy bars. I'd always say I wasn't hungry because I'd eaten a large breakfast. I'd insist only a little food satisfied me. My friends were always too preoccupied to notice what I was eating anyway, which led me to believe this excuse was a good disguise for my bulimia. It seemed to work because they never asked me how I could be so fat, especially if I ate only a couple pretzels and two small cookies for lunch while they ate fried, fatty foods. Surely they figured out I ate when they weren't around, but at least that was better than facing the humiliation I'd suffer if I actually ate like they did in front of them.

By masking my real self from my classmates, I could make it through the day without drawing negative attention, or any attention, to myself. Most people who were not in my immediate class wouldn't even know who I was, as evidenced by the time years later when I ran into someone and they didn't remember me from Monte Vista. Obviously, they didn't take notice of the fat girl.

Before school was out for the day I'd start thinking about what I was going to eat as soon as I got home. I checked out mentally long before my last class was finished. My body had begun having anticipatory reactions to my next binge session. While my mom drove me home each day, my pulse would race as I began to sweat, and not just my armpits, but also my back, stomach, and even the backs of my knees.

I didn't know what to make of this. I figured it was just part of my bulimic routine. I felt that from my last class to the finish of my bulimic episode, I was not myself, but someone else pretending to me. I heard one of the girls at school talking about an out-of-body experience. That's it, I thought, I must be having some kind of out-of-body experience when I binge and purge.

I was anxious and frantic, feeling what I imagined a drug withdrawal might be like as I rushed into the kitchen. I didn't want to talk with my mom as she tried to ask me about my day. I was far too consumed in my own world to engage in small talk with her anyway. Discouraged, she'd usually head to her chair or her room and close the door.

I was now in an altered state. I would shut out everything around me. Nobody and nothing mattered. Mentally, emotionally, and physically I was on a specific quest that no one could interrupt. My after-school binge session would begin with my grabbing everything I could find that I considered to be binge food, that is, food that was easy to throw up such as bread, ice-cream, cereal, crackers. If I chose the wrong foods, my throat would feel like I had literally ripped out pieces of it. I also had to select foods that were abundant so what I ate would go unnoticed. After devouring thousands of calories, I'd head to the bathroom, push two fingers down my throat, and watch the "poison" flush down the cold porcelain toilet.

Afterward, I'd feel a certain type of high, like being stoned on drugs. Like any drug high, though, I would come crashing down. After throwing up, I'd feel like I had been beaten. I had no way of understanding that this behavior was my way of coping with my feelings, experiences, and life in general. My bulimic behaviors were, whenever I thought about them in the abstract, some weird fixation I had with eating followed by an overwhelming feeling of guilt, which meant that I'd have no other choice but to throw up.

After my routine, I'd hibernate in my room for hours. I would lie down on my bed, turn on my stereo, and cry and cry until I was numb and could cry no longer. Only then would I come out of this altered state. Once I'd drifted back to reality, I'd try to act like any other normal teen. I'd do my homework after I had calmed down and talk on the phone with friends in the evening. I also convinced myself that if I appeared as normal as possible, my family wouldn't discover I was bulimic.

My mom had, on numerous occasions, pounded on the locked bathroom door, yelling, "Are you throwing up in there?" Or as I left the bathroom, she'd race to catch me and ask to smell my breath and hands. But that is as far as it went. She didn't seek counsel or even talk with me. With no hope of finding support from her, I decided I needed to be more discrete so there would be less chance I'd be discovered for the abnormal, crazy person I believed I was.

A year had passed since my first encounter with Diet Center and any diet I invented for myself after hadn't worked, except for the starve-yourself-into-mono diet. My mom persuaded me to try another type of weight loss program, a highly publicized hypnotist. I reluctantly agreed to go because I was ashamed I hadn't lost any weight since regaining the forty-six pounds. One Saturday morning, she and I went to the Holiday Inn in San Francisco where I met the hypnotist face to face. Once we arrived and I completed all the necessary paperwork and paid the three-hundred-dollar fee for the seminar plus additional money for his tapes, I was told to take a seat in a huge meeting room that, to my surprise, was filled with hundreds of other very hopeless and desperate overweight people searching for some miracle that would change their lives.

I wasn't ready for this experience and didn't believe that some stranger could cure me of my secret disease and addiction to food. What was my mom thinking when she signed me up for this? Did she think this big, scary-looking man with a deep voice preaching a load of garbage to me and the rest of the audience was going to instantly take us all under his hypnotic spell and make us better? Even I knew this man couldn't solve my problems.

My mom had once again convinced herself that this would be the solution to her problem with my size and my overeating and had spent money we couldn't spare. The pressure and guilt I felt because of this made it impossible for me to object to her proposals. As I watched the big man trying to "preach the fat out of me," I couldn't help but find myself drifting off into space. At fourteen, I certainly wasn't feeling the "power of his words." Once again I felt like I was already doomed for failure.

Once the session was over and I saw the hopeful look in my mother's eyes, I told her it was good and I felt confident I was going to lose weight and get skinny again. The whole experience sunk in for me as we headed home. I had just been reduced to attending some very weird session that made me feel like more of a nut than I already did.

Naturally, I didn't get hypnotized during the session and felt nothing in terms of being moved. But having spent several hundred dollars on all the mantras he had visited upon me and the rest of the desperate men and women in the audience, none of whom were anywhere near my age, I tried to read his book and listen to his tapes, hoping for a miracle. I felt nothing, ever. Months passed as I pretended to my mom that this diet program was going to work. I knew I had failed and this diet was a farce. Just like last year with my experience at Diet Center and my very own diet, I failed again. Three diets in less than a year and a half … and three big failures.

My mom had faith in the hypnotist and his bag of tricks, so she decided to accelerate my weight loss path further by buying me some exercise equipment. With that in mind, we headed to Walnut Creek in her blue Oldsmobile. I felt guilty and dishonest because I knew the tapes weren't working, and I wasn't excited at all about having to buy exercise equipment. I thought my mom was repeating with actions, rather than words, her opinion that, "If you'd only lose weight, then you'd be happy."

What that meant to me was, "Jocelyn, you are no good unless you lose weight and quit being a fat kid." I was embarrassed having to walk into an exercise equipment store, especially because the guy assisting us looked like a mini version of Arnold Schwarzenegger. I felt dumpier than ever before. My mom proceeded to tell Arnold Junior about how I was working on losing weight, and he suggested that a stationary bike would be best for me. It would go downstairs in my bedroom where I could use it all the time.

How unattractive the whole situation seemed to me. But as always, I tried to put on a brave face and mimic my mother's enthusiasm. "Yes, the Tunturi bike looks great. I can see myself using it," I lied, unable to focus on anything other than how this guy must have thought I was a tub-of-lard.

We bought the Tunturi bicycle. I wondered why my mom didn't see how humiliated I felt standing in front of the bodybuilder guy looking like a fat freak who's very own mother was unhappy with her? Couldn't she see how much she was hurting me by constantly trying to find the miracle solution that would make me skinny? Didn't she love me for me? I knew that answer. No. It was loud and clear just as it always had been.

Reluctantly I pedaled away for thirty, sometimes forty-five, minutes a day while listening to the hypnotic tapes my mom bought me. I tried this routine for months—I'd either bike before school or before dinner—but I never lost any weight. I knew I was binging and purging far too much and in such huge quantities that no bike, not even the most expensive one in the world, was going to help me lose weight. I withdrew deeper and deeper, and food began to move from simple comfort to surrogate mother.

At school I remained shy and found it difficult to talk to even my very best friend when I was feeling blue. Stacy would constantly try to help me and get out whatever it was that was bothering me. But I knew I could only reveal so much to her or anyone else, and I couldn't risk anyone at Monte Vista becoming privy to my eating disorder. I wanted to tell her everything, but I'd get tongue-tied every time I tried.

On the other hand, Monica became more and more of an unwelcome friend, crueler than any stranger. I already knew back in junior high how cruel she could be, but as she grew up, her behavior grew worse. Right in the middle of the quad area where we'd all hang out during break, Monica would measure me up from top to bottom and roll her eyes, indicating she was disgusted with my appearance. That was embarrassing enough, because she always did her little eye work when others were around, but she didn't stop there. She started to call me names when we were eating together. The times I decided I was too hungry for just my bag of pretzels and Fig-Newtons, I would grab a salad, thinking I was at least making a healthy food choice. But this made no difference to Monica. She would call me a "fat cow" or "pig" right to my face and laugh as she humiliated me. Every time she called me those embarrassing and hurtful names, I would bite my tongue as hard as I could, to hold back the tears. I'm sure she knew how much it hurt, and that's why she did it. Throughout high school Monica continued to humiliate me, right up until the day I graduated.

When freshman year finally came to an end, I was grateful I made it through alive. Oftentimes, I wished I hadn't. I hated Monte Vista. I hated feeling so crappy about myself all the time. And I hated the fact that my own family didn't like me because I was too fat. I felt defeated and didn't hold much hope for things to improve.

Sophomore year presented another dreaded year of attending Monte Vista. Each day was predictable—binge and purge, binge and purge, binge and purge. I wasn't getting better. I was getting worse. I still weighed roughly one hundred fifty pounds so, naturally, trying to look cute in my new school clothes was an impossible task and facing another year of being surrounded by the rich and beautiful didn't appeal to me much either.

Since my stint with the hypnotist had proved to be a complete waste of time and money, my mom was still as persistent as ever in finding a way for me to lose weight. To my amazement, she decided I would go back to Diet Center. She would say I agreed to this decision. Perhaps I did, but in reality, I wanted her to love me for me and not on the condition I earn her love by losing weight. Just a few weeks after school started, we headed off to that horrible little building behind Burger King where the same little old lady created my new chart, weighed me, and led us to the little Diet Center grocery store. I felt like I was returning to a prison cell after a couple years of freedom. With a reluctant smile, I pretended enthusiasm about rejoining the program. I was fifteen now and felt whatever little sense of independence or confidence I had was being stripped away. Once again I was the diet slave, shackled and chained by my own body and the expectations of those around me.

Again the same routine of going to Diet Center to get weighed, feeling the utter humiliation as I stared at the scale telling me how fat I actually was, and going home pretending to my mom I was motivated. Every time I had to step on the scale, I was demoralized and demotivated. I wanted to turn to food to feel some level of comfort. I tried to follow the program. But this time, unlike the attempt in junior high, I didn't stick to it. I binged and purged every day and only when I wasn't eating everything I could get my hands on, would I try to eat the dry, tasteless, powdery food.

The first week, I lost a pound and half, the second week no weight at all. By now I was very creative in terms of making up excuses as to why I wasn't losing weight. I had enough practice that I could just roll some bogus excuse right off the tip of my tongue and not think twice about it. We continued to spend hundreds of dollars over the next few weeks while I faked my compliance to the program. My mom was discouraged by my failure to lose weight. She was forking out the money, but the return on her investment just wasn't there. I finally told her I couldn't continue. She argued with me and tried to dissuade me from quitting. Her unspoken message told me I had failed her, that I wasn't good enough as I was. In return I just ate and ate to numb my feelings and learned to close my heart down little by little.

One day, after Carolyn was married and Susan was off at college, my parents announced they could no longer tolerate sleeping in the same room with each other. There was no real marriage beyond a tattered certificate, but still this news came as a shock to me. I never heard of married couples splitting up but continuing to live in the same house. Years later someone would refer to this as the "Catholic divorce," which is exactly what it was, i.e., to all intents and purposes split up, live separate lives, but don't divorce because it's a sin.

I found this arrangement very upsetting. It confirmed for me my feeling that my parents had in reality always lived separate lives. How could my mom and dad think this crazy way of living wasn't going to affect me? How could their severing direct contact with each other not make living in the house intolerable for me? I knew of no one with this absurd arrangement. Wouldn't this just be the icing on the cake for those who already thought we were a crazy, dysfunctional, anti-social family? My parents never had company, never went out together, and the family as a unit never did either. We were finally providing overt evidence of what I figured most people already assumed.

The move was for real and now my parents could begin what would eventually be like a divorce that stopped short of the finishing line. My mom had her TV and her phone in her new room, my dad still watched TV in the family room, and they never had to spend time with each other. Ever since I could remember, I wanted a mom and dad who loved each other and who loved their kids. Now my dreams of being part of a happy and loving family were forever squashed.

I feared my friend, Stacy, would discover that my mom and dad no longer slept in the same room. Of course she did eventually ask and feeling humiliated, I told her my parents didn't want to be in the same room together any longer. I proceeded to tell Stacy—like she didn't already sense my family had problems—that my parents weren't "married." She knew they never did anything together as a married couple, unlike her family, and she knew my parents had some issues. She stumbled across this new arrangement one night when sleeping over and not knowing how to react, she was a true friend and didn't make me feel worse by questioning me about the revelation that my parents no longer wanted to be together. Separate but together? How could that possibly lead to a positive outcome? I never got over the bizarre arrangement. Divorce is far more preferable than living two separate lives under the same roof.

As the reshuffling of rooms was completed, my mom remained true to her colors. She spent most her days battling feelings of fatigue, tiredness, and depression while my dad was off in his own world. My relationship with him never improved. Rather as I grew up, we couldn't have been further apart. He never once engaged in anything I did, let alone talk to me about my likes, dislikes, or life in general. No, my dad and I were complete strangers. What I knew about him remained the same as always. He had a temper and I didn't want to be a part of it. Besides, now I knew he liked only skinny people, so having him actually like me, his own daughter, was out of the question. I was fat, therefore, I was unlikable.

Chapter 10

The Dying Game

My ticket to freedom arrived on September 26, 1984, my sixteenth birthday. Now I had access to a car and could use it whenever I needed. I could practice my bulimia wherever I wanted. I was now able to live by my own schedule and I'd had no rules to follow since starting high school. By then my parents were drained from dealing with my two sisters. I didn't even have a curfew and I could skip school. My mom would write me notes excusing me for some bogus reason, and I could pretty much do what I wanted. I could come and go and binge and purge as I pleased.

My newfound freedom did not come without consequence. My relationship with bulimia spiraled ever further downward as my ability and opportunity to practice it increased. I was far more violent and self-destructive than I had been since beginning at thirteen. Now I had become so involved in my bulimia that it jaded everything else in my life. I went through the motions of growing up. I went to school, unless I cut class, did my homework, and tried to enjoy myself outside our home. But I was at a standstill emotionally and not able to mature the way a non-bulimic would. I didn't embrace life or learn how to deal with the challenges I faced. I lacked any useful skills or knowledge that would help me develop into a productive and confident teenager. Without knowing it, I stunted my emotional growth, ensuring that I didn't mature the way my friends and peers did. I focused my attention on filling, at least briefly, the loveless void I felt the only way I knew how—by binging and purging.

My sixteenth birthday marked further isolation from the world so I could concentrate fully on my relationship with bulimia. I rarely went straight home from school to do my homework, let alone go over to a friend's house to hang out. Instead, I'd pack all my belongings and embark on my biggest bulimic ritual of the day. I'd tear out of the parking lot and drive from store to store—Lucky's Supermarket, Safeway, 7-Eleven, and Winchell's Donuts—and then from fast-food restaurant to fast-food restaurant—Burger King, Wendy's,

Taco Bell—where I'd buy and eat as much sugary and greasy fried food as I possibly could. I put piles of candy and cookies on the register counter and ordered combo meals at every restaurant. If the checkout clerk asked me any questions, I'd always lie and say my mom was having company and she asked me to pick up sweets for the guests. I would pray every day as I waited to pay for my binge food that I wouldn't run into anyone I knew. What would I say to them? I was fat and surely they wouldn't believe the same lie I'd tell the check-out person. I never once ran into anyone I knew. Besides, what teen did I know who would spend the afternoon shopping for binge food? After all, nobody else was like me.

Because I was frantic and petrified about discovery, I would eat all the food I had just purchased while I drove to my next destination. Then before I'd either park or drive up to the drive-through window of my next stop to pay for whatever enormous meal I was ordering, I would toss all the wrappers from my last stop under my car seat to make sure nobody discovered the food I had moments before shoved down my throat.

My erratic driving mimicked that of a drunk driver except I wasn't under the influence of alcohol. I was under the influence of the high I got from binging. I would ignore the rules of the road, run red lights, dodge across parking lots in an unsafe manner, speed, and swerve in and out of lanes. Basically I did anything I felt I had to do to get to the next destination as quickly as possible and then get home. I cared more about the threat of not being able to throw up all the "bad" food I just ate, than potentially hurting someone or even myself in a car accident. My complete fear of getting even fatter was nearly unbearable. Getting bigger was almost like having a death sentence bestowed on me, yet I'd sooner die than get fatter.

I needed reassurance that I didn't digest any of the calories I'd just eaten, so I devised a very private and intricate way of determining if I had eliminated everything. I decided I would use the real throw-up can in the upstairs bathroom closet to purge. Because the throw-up can allowed me to measure my food output versus input, it enabled me to feel like I had control and assurance that I got rid of everything. By using the throw-up can, I could sift through the disgusting contents and search for remnants. Until I was completely convinced that I expelled everything, I would continue to try and make myself through up until absolutely nothing but stomach bile emerged. Once I completed this ritual, I'd further need to determine if I was ready to call it quits by weighing the throw-up can on the bathroom scale. For some reason, I felt it must weigh no less than two pounds. I computed this by calculating the amount of food I'd eaten. Usually I was looking for it to weigh in the region of three or four pounds. Only then could I, little by little, dump the contents into the toilet and watch it all get flushed away.

This violent way of throwing up inevitably left me weak and unbalanced. Once I finished throwing up, my face would turn completely white and I would become light-headed. Sweat would drip down my forehead, the sides of my cheeks, and down the middle of my back. Worse than merely sweating or feeling like I was going to faint from severe light-headedness, my body and hands would shake uncontrollably. I knew something, possibly my electrolytes, were out of whack. Most times I could barely stand after the ordeal, so I would lie on the cold, tile bathroom floor. This cooled me off and by resting for a bit, I could regain my energy. The bigger the binge the longer my recovery process took, often totaling nearly a half hour before I could breathe new life into myself and leave the bathroom.

After my afternoon bulimic episode, I would retreat to my bedroom, turn on some music, and do my usual crying until the tears ran dry. I felt worthless, just as useless as a piece of trash. I didn't care about myself and what the future had in store for me. I just wanted to disappear so I wouldn't have to repeat the ritual tomorrow. I began praying fanatically again, hoping that this time around God would hear me recite those special Novenas. Only now I would include the option of not waking up after I went to sleep, so I would no longer feel such pain.

I knew I was getting worse. In my junior year of high school I felt incredibly alone. I realized my behavior was not normal and not something I was willing to reveal to anyone, especially anyone I knew at Monte Vista. I was ashamed of developing an out-of-control fixation with food, and I worried people would think I was out of my mind, that I was crazy. I didn't know bulimia wasn't about simply wanting or feeling the need to consume huge amounts of food, that its true nature was about deep-seated troubles in which the disease takes control to protect, preserve, and even provide comfort to the sufferer. Understanding "why" I had bulimia would take me years and years to figure out. For now, though, I just knew I wasn't normal and something was very wrong with me.

My mom had a couple years of being suspicious, but she never pursued her hunch any further than ragging at me about what I was eating or sometimes waiting outside the bathroom and asking to smell my hands and breath. Her intervention only went that far. I wish she had said she loved me just the way I was and that maybe it would be a good idea if we got some help in understanding my true feelings. She never did.

I felt the pressures of not being popular. I already had many years under my belt walking around feeling less of a person and not worthy of anything. I decided that because the real me was too fat and ugly to look at, I had to cover up and disguise myself as best as I could. Shoulder pads were in style that year. I firmly believed wearing them in absolutely every shirt, blouse, and sweater I owned would help me de-emphasize my shape. I bought all kinds and thought the bigger the better. What I didn't realize was, because I was overweight and had developed huge breasts, the shoulder pads made me look even bigger. I was like a female linebacker. To round things off, I wore so much makeup that I often got teased by people at school, sometimes even by people I didn't know. I wore at least three different colors of eye shadow on my lids, layers and layers of black mascara, gobs of foundation to cover the blemishes that would pop up every month or so from all the greasy makeup, and dark, nearly black, lipstick. I felt if anyone saw the real me, with little to no makeup on, they would simply be frightened. I hated the way I looked, and I thought it was better to be teased about wearing too much makeup than being exposed as ugly and having people reject the real me. At least that way, I could try and mask who I was. Every morning as I put on my many layers of clothing and makeup, I was trying to hide not only from the outside world but from myself as well.

Given my rather bizarre look and my large frame, it is maybe not surprising that no boy showed interest in me since I'd started at Monte Vista. I was convinced no guy would want to be seen with me. It would be too embarrassing. It wasn't like Monte Vista didn't have many, many beautiful and slim girls. Whenever I'd hang out with guys, I was always the friend of a friend and mostly I seemed invisible to them. They would talk to my girlfriends but would almost never look directly at me or say anything to me. Thus far, I hadn't been asked to go to any after-school parties or any of the many formal dances, like homecoming, the Christmas dance, and, soon, the junior prom. I dreaded it when all the guys and girls gossiped about whom they were going to ask to the dances or who would be their date. All my friends got asked well in advance, just as they'd expected. I'd put on a brave face and pretend that not being asked didn't bother me. Of course it did. For weeks I'd feel like I was more of a loser than I already believed I was. I could only hope that the big event would come and go as quickly as possible. I buried my feelings inside, seeking comfort in food. I binged and purged just as hard, if not harder, than when I first got my driver's license.

Monte Vista was a very rich, highly competitive high school in Contra Costa County, and nearly everyone came from money or seemed to have money. My family fell somewhere in the middle class, but in the East Bay and especially at Monte Vista High, money and family status were very important and had a direct impact on peer acceptance. We had the necessities—a house, a car, food, clothing, and even a little to spare—but even so, we seemed to have far less as a family than the typical kid at my high school. I didn't mind because I never put too much store into having the material possessions the kids in my area had. I was far too consumed with my bulimia to waste too much time and energy caring. Nonetheless it solidified my low-ranking position on the teen popularity charts. My looks didn't further that or peer acceptance and neither did my possessions. While most students drove cars like Honda CRXs, Volkswagon GTIs, BMWs, and even Porsches to Monte Vista, I drove my mother's beat-up, dented, blue Oldsmobile. I knew I was fortunate to have a car to use, but I always felt like a geek driving it around. What mattered at my high school were looks and material possessions, including cars and clothes. I lost in both categories. I felt like I had been doomed from the start.

Since I had my driver's license, it was time I got a job. I had no work skills and looking the way I looked, my pickings were slim. I applied for all kinds of crappy jobs: a cashier at a paint store, a check-in clerk at a launderette, a receptionist, even a phone solicitor. Eventually I got a job at probably one of the worst places for me, a small, privately owned, fast-food restaurant. I was desperate and needed money, so I didn't take into account the impact being surrounded by greasy, fattening food would have on my bulimia. Chicago Hotdog Company was not too far away from either school or home, and I was relieved to have been given a job. There was no mistaking the fact that I didn't get the many jobs I applied for because I looked like a fat, painted freak and few people wanted me being the first person the customer would see. But at the Chicago Hotdog Company, this didn't seem to matter. I'd be responsible for all facets of the job, from cooking and serving to cleaning and cashiering. What I liked best of all was that I could wear whatever clothes I wanted, so at least I didn't have to feel like an oversized weirdo in some ugly bright red and orange uniform.

It didn't take long for me to feel comfortable enough to sneak food here and there. Naturally I didn't want to pig out in front of my coworkers, but I was pretty good at taking a bit of food and not being noticed. I could walk to the back of the restaurant and secretly shove French fries or a chocolate chip cookie down my throat without fear of detection. I'd even put food in my pockets and go to the bathroom to secretly eat my stash. In my heart, I knew this job was only allowing my addiction to run rampant, but I had no other alternatives and I needed money. Sometimes I felt like an alcoholic working in a bar, but I was a food-aholic working in a greasy, fast-food joint. Within just a few months, I could feel my clothes getting tighter and tighter. Even though I continued to throw up mornings, after the lunch rush, and at night, the calories I was adding to my diet were inevitably causing me to gain weight. I didn't know what I could do to help myself. I couldn't do much on my own. I'd already failed miserably at diet program after diet program and certainly I couldn't go to my mom, let alone my dad so I reached for the comforts food brought me. It was a vicious cycle, and I had no clue how to stop or get out. Before long, I had packed on a solid ten pounds and I was now somewhere around the one-hundred-sixty-pound mark. I was just as fat as ever and nothing seemed to help me lose weight. This was a result of my ever more intense bulimia, but at the same time I needed it now more than ever and couldn't imagine my life without it.

Despite having participated in many diets by now, I had little real knowledge of nutrition. I had simply followed whatever diet I was on, but I was never taught about nutrition or overall health. Whenever my dad felt like snacking or he didn't make it to the coffee shop, he'd opt for all types of fatty foods like sweet rolls, bear claws, Danishes—which he smothered with clumps of butter—and fried eggs. My mom barely ate anything, so she didn't have a weight problem. Quite the opposite, she was very slim. I was getting all kinds of mixed messages when it came to food. Look at all the greasy fatty foods I can eat, but not you, you'll get fat. Or, just don't eat and then you will be slim like me. Or, eat only these types of foods and then you will lose weight. I was so confused by now that I didn't have a clue what foods were actually good for me and important to eat for proper nutrition. To make some sense out of my constant battle, I relied on bulimia to help me so I could eat like my family and friends, yet be thin like my mom.

Sports weren't something my parents participated in or watched. Susan was a great athlete, but even so, I never understood the connection between exercise and weight. I swam for many years and knew that participating in some type of activity was better than none at all. For whatever reason, though, I wasn't able to grasp the full concept of cardiovascular fitness and burning calories. I was surviving the best way I knew how. Unfortunately for me, my way of surviving wasn't working very well.

I still attempted diet after diet even during my tenure at Chicago Hotdog Company. I felt terrible about myself because I gained weight even though I threw up daily. And when I was working, I couldn't throw up because the place was too small, I worked with at least one to two people at a time, and customers were always coming and going. It was no surprise I gained weight, eating all the junk food that I did.

In desperation, I decided to try the very popular liquid diets sold at every drug and grocery store around. The Cambridge Diet was relatively new, but the ads promised great results. I went to the local Thrifty store down in Alamo and bought a container of the Cambridge powder. The chocolate flavor seemed most appealing, so I walked up to the checkout counter with my big container of Cambridge, and though I was embarrassed to be admitting my problem to the cashier and everyone else in line, I proceeded to pay the lady and embark on yet another diet program.

After buying my chocolate-flavored powder, I went home and headed straight to my room. As I sat on my bed listening to Pat Benatar on my record player, I read and re-read the instructions for using the liquid diet. I hoped I was going to somehow miraculously shed all the weight I needed to and pushed aside any feelings of defeat for the moment. I allowed myself to concentrate only on how I was going to lose lots of weight by drinking the supposedly tasty drink. I was feeling pretty positive I'd succeed because I paid for this diet myself and I didn't have to go into some awkward clinic with a little old lady and my mom hovering over the scale then looking horrified at my weight. The next morning, instead of eating my usual huge breakfast, which I would throw up anyway, I put the two scoops of Cambridge powder into the blender, added water, and blended away. As I took my first sip, I cringed. All the Cambridge ads promised a delicious and nutritious liquid diet, but they lied. It tasted like liquefied cardboard with a faint hint of chocolate.

Still, I wasn't going to give up that easily. I had endured enough dreadful diet experiences so far that I had the will to give this one its fair chance. I finished my drink and made another one to bring to school in a thermos. My friends saw it at lunchtime and asked me what it was. I was humiliated when I had to tell them it was a liquid diet. On top of that, I never got used to the taste. I tried and tried, day after day, to drink the diet swamp water, but to no avail. I didn't lose any more than a few pounds.

Working at Chicago Hotdog Company four to five times a week didn't help. If I wasn't trying to gulp down the horrible drink, I was gorging and purging on anything I could find. I knew this wasn't a good combination and it would not be the magic solution I craved. My mom knew too. After several weeks, I could no longer stand to drink the Cambridge diet. By now, I had chalked up four real diet programs with basically no success. Instead, I wasted money and, more importantly, these diets continued to beat me down emotionally and physically and reinforced my belief I was a failure and confirm I was destined for a pathetic and lonely life.

After watching me fail with the Cambridge Diet, my mom did a little research and came across NutriSystem, the latest diet program to hit America. Within a few weeks of quitting the Cambridge Diet, my mom made me an appointment with a NutriSystem diet counselor. I didn't fully understand what was going on with me physically, let alone emotionally, so I bought into everything either my family told me or what I heard while in school. I wanted more than anything to be accepted and loved. I was willing to do whatever it took to get that. Because my mom thought NutriSystem would be the best thing way for me to lose weight, I convinced myself that maybe it would work. What I learned immediately was that NutriSystem was very similar to Diet Center, only the facility itself was much classier.

Once the meeting was confirmed, my mom and I drove to Concord where I met with a counselor who weighed me in a little back room. I was just as mortified, if not more so, than at Diet Center. There were far more clients and workers and just being in the presence of the slim and beautiful counselors and weight specialist made me feel like a big, fat, humiliated elephant. I was ashamed and very embarrassed to get on the scale and see it read one hundred sixty-one pounds. My mom was standing right beside me while the attractive, very petite counselor recorded all my vital information and my weight in my personal folder. I wanted to run out of the building right then and never go back. It felt too much like Diet Center but more intense. I was no longer excited. I was demoralized. I was fat. I stood there not knowing what to say or do, pretending the whole experience wasn't happening.

After we left the weigh-in room, the counselor recommended I sit in on a small behavior modification session with about five other women. The counselor was leading a discussion about her weight-loss experience. I wasn't about to share that I was a terribly insecure, fat sixteen-year-old with a serious food addiction. I stared into space then after the session ended, followed the counselor to another room and bought a variety of NutriSystem food to take home and eat for the week. The choices were better than Diet Center's, but in the end it was pretty much the same dried, prepackaged, powdery foods requiring water, or the tiniest crackers, thirteen of which constituted a serving. I wasn't excited, but knew I couldn't let my mom or the counselor know how I felt.

My mom and I left NutriSystem and went straight home where I unpacked the week's food. Most of what I was going to have was in powder form, and I cringed at the thought of adding only hot water to the package and calling it a meal. But I was committed, especially because I felt like I couldn't disappoint my parents again. They were spending their money, and it seemed my losing weight mattered more to them than anything else about me. Plus NutriSystem was more expensive than Diet Center, so I felt additional pressure to be successful.

I bit my tongue and hoped through osmosis I'd be able to make a success of this diet program. I followed it religiously for the first week. Once the week was over my food was gone, a very clever scheme to keep clients coming back and spending money. I had my weigh-in appointment to see what progress the scale said I'd made. Because I felt pressured by my mom and guilty about the money my parents had spent, I was able to restrict myself to only three bulimic sessions that week, a landmark for me.

Off to Concord we went and within just a few minutes of arriving, the thin counselor called me to come to the back room where I knew I'd humiliate myself. Instead, I'd lost four and three quarter pounds. I was so happy. I felt I had pleased my mom. I knew I was still fat and had a long road ahead of me, but when my mom bought another week's supply of their food, I tried to muster up the enthusiasm and courage to continue.

I knew immediately after leaving the facility that this week was going to be much harder for me than the previous one. Again I had to bring some of the pre-packaged food to school for lunch, which utterly embarrassed me. Not only did my friends know I was participating in the NutriSystem diet, but anyone in my vicinity in the cafeteria became privy to this information as well. It was impossible for me to hide and eat in solitude. I was so hungry that I ate whatever the diet allowed me to have for lunch, but I was ashamed of the little packets of food boldly labeled with the NutriSystem logo. They made me feel as though I was shouting to the world I knew I was fat and I couldn't eat like others because I had to have special fat-people food.

I started feeling worn out from the nearly four years of severe dieting and violent bulimia. Day by day I was finding it more and more difficult to eat the NutriSystem food and worried about what would happen once I went back to regular food. I already knew from first-hand experience that if I deviated from whatever diet specifics I was supposed to follow, I would gain weight. I thought this would be yet another failed attempt. It was. I gained weight by the third week and resumed my bulimic rituals day and night. Secretly I knew I could no longer handle the humiliation I felt, especially at school in front of my classmates. I wanted to secretly diet rather than reveal to the world that I was dieting. I wanted to try and lose weight my own way and to stop throwing up everyday. I couldn't tell my mom this, so I made up another excuse. With obvious disappointment, she allowed me to quit the NutriSystem diet.

During summer break I continued to work at Chicago Hotdog Company and to secretly eat food during my shifts. I somehow managed to not gain any more weight, just the ten pounds that seemed like they were here to stay, but that made no difference to my feelings about myself. I worked more hours since I wasn't attending school and with my new schedule, I could feel my weight. I was much hotter than my coworkers, sweating all the time. I was embarrassed because I knew that overweight people sweat more, and, as usual, sought comfort in food. I finally felt as if I couldn't work around food any longer and made the decision to look for another job. This time I hoped my job search would be easier, because I'd had a job for nearly a year now and did good work despite feeling crummy about myself.

My search didn't last long, and I accepted a position at the City of Shoes. I would sell shoes to all customers—men, women, and children. I was happy not to have to face tempting food while trying to work. The summer passed quickly and before I knew it, it was time to go back to school for my senior year. I was now seventeen and starting what should have been the best year of my high school life, but by then I was in the depths of my bulimia—binging anywhere from three to five thousand calories per episode, three to five times a day. My face was constantly swollen and several small capillary veins in my cheeks had popped from all the blood rushing to my head when I bent over to force out food. My body ached from head to toe, and I continuously felt fatigued and beaten. I also had severe stomach pains that would only increase with time.

Although I had been binging and purging since eighth grade, my mom, despite having some suspicions about my throwing up, continued to put pressure on me to lose weight. She and my dad—he by ignoring me or signaling with negative body language—still treated me like a fat person and to them a fat person was not a worthy person. Two months into my new classes, my mom, who never gave up researching miracle cures for her daughter's horrible affliction, stumbled across another means for me to lose weight. This time I would be seeing a diet psychologist. I don't think my mom ever let go of the whole hypnotism thing and believed that this could work for me if I worked at it hard enough. My private visits with the shrink became my next diet undertaking. Reluctantly, I went off the following Wednesday afternoon to meet with my new savior, the diet shrink, Dr. Laura. She had a practice in Quail Creek business park in Walnut Creek, just fifteen minutes up the freeway from my home in Alamo, so it was very convenient according to my mother. Great, we can go there all the time, I thought, at once sarcastic and despondent.

Dr. Laura was one of the tallest and thinnest ladies I had ever seen. She must have been nearly six feet tall and was obviously anorexic. She was so thin she reminded me of Olive Oyl, Popeye's girlfriend. I couldn't believe my eyes. I wasn't sure whether to laugh or cry when it occurred to me that my mom had hooked up me, the fat bulimic, with an anorexic psychologist. Unbelievable.

I sat in the patient chair, overweight, wearing big clothes and lots of makeup, and instead of talking as a patient would normally do when seeing a therapist, I sat there listening to this string bean ramble on. Dr. Laura talked for the full hour mostly in the abstract. It all went in one ear and out the other. It seemed to me she had her own set of issues going on. At the end of the session, she gave me a diet workbook and special guidelines to follow for eating. Dr. Laura was so skinny that all I took away from the session was how opposite we were. I figured all I could learn from her would be how to swap bulimia for full-blown anorexia.

Afterwards, my mom diligently reviewed with me what the good doctor had recommended I do in terms of my food intake. But I was turned off and had no confidence in this program. I couldn't tell my mom, though, because I felt so guilty she'd spent three hundred dollars for just one session. What a rip-off, I thought. Instead of being inspired by a therapist, I was discouraged and felt worse than before. I was fat and bulimic and my therapist was tall and anorexic. In all aspects, physically and emotionally, we were on completely different pages. I couldn't relate to her and because Dr. Laura seemed so fragile herself, I found it a challenge to believe anything she was telling me. I made my best attempt to follow her guidelines. I tried to eat only what she told me I could, but two days after our meeting, I resorted to my only comfort and relief, a binge and purge rampage. I threw up nonstop that entire blurry week. I felt ashamed that I'd let my mom down and didn't lose any weight.

I went to see Dr. Laura one more time and after that I never returned. Once again, I had to figure out a way to break the news to my mom that this diet wasn't going to work for me. And once again, I had to look into her eyes and see her acute disappointment.

Not only had I now spent the last five years overweight, but my chest had grown so much my cup size exceeded a double-D. Although I refused to buy a bra any larger than a double-D, I know now my breasts were more like an E or F. I was so embarrassed and tried everything I could think of to cover up. Being fat was bad enough, but now I had to deal with breasts well beyond the size of any other senior in my class, or anyone else I had ever seen for that matter. I felt entirely defeated. Because my breasts were so out of proportion, too big even for my oversized body, I usually wore my bra to bed every night. If I didn't, the pain I felt when not strapped in was far worse than just letting my breasts hang loose. Each morning I would wake up and have deep, sore, red marks where my bra straps had dug into my flesh underneath my breasts and on my shoulders. Even my weight fluctuations never affected my chest, which seemed to have its own growth patterns.

As time passed, I grew sick of enduring the pain I felt from lugging around my extra large breasts. One day while an acquaintance and I were commiserating, she shared with me that she had gone to a surgeon who performed a breast reduction on her and she was thrilled with the results. That evening, as my mom sat in her favorite chair, I told her of Sarah's news. She called the surgeon and scheduled an appointment.

Both she and I were nervous about the whole thing, but we had mutually decided if I passed the insurance tests regarding their covering the costs—they only do so if it is absolutely necessary—then we would go ahead with the surgery. The severity of the pain in my back, shoulders, and my chest, my inability to participate in certain activities due to the restraints of an oversized chest, and so on, qualified me for coverage. Within just a few weeks, we received the news that the insurance company would cover the entire cost, minus a small co-pay. We decided I would have the surgery.

My mom and I agreed the best time for me to have the surgery was at Thanksgiving. That way, I could take time out for the bed rest I would need and also, we hoped, return to school with a renewed sense of self. Before the actual surgery, the doctor made me commit to losing as much weight as I possibly could. I cut out as many calories as possible and tried to binge and purge only what I knew for sure would come up, leaving no hidden calories for my body to digest. They photographed me from every possible angle. I was horrified when I viewed the naked, waist-up photos of my huge, saggy breasts and rolls of fat on my back and front. Looking in the mirror is one thing, but the photos revolted me. I was inspired to make a change in my life. I had no idea, though, that this surgery would be the vehicle that opened up doors for me and a new way of living.

Prior to the big day, I managed to lose six pounds. That was all I could accomplish given that my surgery was scheduled in just two weeks. Under the knife I went and off came the huge breasts. As scared as I was about what was undoubtedly the biggest decision I had made in my seventeen years, I somehow knew I had to do this. I couldn't visualize myself having small breasts, but after seeing the many photographs of other patients, I hoped everything would turn out okay.

Once the surgery was over and I returned home, I felt a huge weight had been lifted—literally! When I looked down, I could see the tips of my toes, if I sucked in my stomach. I was wrapped in gauze for several days and in a good deal of pain, but I felt like I was becoming a new person. When I returned to school the next week, everyone thought I'd lost an incredible amount of weight. My body and the way I presented myself changed overnight. It seemed on the surface as if I'd lost fifteen to twenty pounds. I did lose more weight due to the surgery, medication, and emotional exhaustion, somewhere shy of thirteen pounds, which was huge for me. But my big, uneven, saggy chest was gone. Soon my oversized shirts with big shoulder pads would go away too. For the moment, this new body gave me a glimmer of hope, and I felt for the first time as if I had a glimpse of what it was like to be seen as a person and not a big, fat teen with huge breasts.

After my surgery, I changed my strategy about the food choices I made. I embarked on a much more intensive relationship with myself and my bulimia. I was determined to lose weight because, unlike before, I now had the ability to move my body freely. I wanted to be thin more than anything. Being thin was the only way I could see my life changing.

With six months to graduation, my breast reduction sparked new insight and a new confidence. I was better able to choose whether to binge and purge or stop eating all together—actually I'd consume about four hundred fifty calories a day. This combination proved more successful than any diet I had tried in the past. When I partied with my friends, I would allow myself to eat like they did, but only for that night. Otherwise, I did not snack between my binge and purge sessions, and with the help of diet supplements like Dexatrim, I didn't feel hungry. I added into my daily caloric allowance those foods that remained inside of me, those I couldn't throw up because it was impossible to get rid of every single morsel. This clever method worked for me and, gradually, I began to shed pounds. I continued with the nightmare of food-store hopping, diet pill popping, and the occasional laxative use that had started senior year, in combination with starving myself. I had found a successful weight loss program I would continue to use from here on, unwittingly damaging myself physically and emotionally.

Graduation was nearing and I had managed to drop enough weight—I reached one hundred thirty-two pounds—to wear a size eight dress very comfortably. As I lost weight, my classmates began to want to hang out with me but I was no longer interested in making these false friendships. I'd been deeply hurt by their shunning me when I was overweight. Instead I focused on my life outside Monte Vista. Now that I could wear a size eight, I felt a little more confident and hopeful about my future. Instead of going to the high school parties, which I hated anyway, my friends and I would go to UC Berkeley on weekends and party with the college boys.

For the very first time in my life, I was enjoying myself and felt a sense of calm because anyone who met me in Berkeley had no idea who I was and where I came from. I cut classes all the time and was rarely at school. I had taken advanced classes since the seventh grade, so before my senior year, I had completed most everything I needed to graduate. I took several teacher's aid classes, gym, and typing to pass my days and the three classes required to graduate. I had a car, a few friends, and no desire to be at Monte Vista all day. I would cut class and head off in the morning or afternoon or sometimes all day. I just didn't care anymore. I missed so much school during my four years at Monte Vista that I had the third worst attendance record in my entire class of four hundred fifty students. Despite being interested in learning, cutting class was preferable so I could avoid being in Monte Vista and facing the ridicule of the rich and pretty. I still managed to get good grades, all A's and B's and the odd C, despite my poor attendance, because I always did my lessons and studied twice as hard as anyone I knew for exams. My mom never said anything about my cutting school as long as I kept up my marks; that was all that mattered. She didn't seem too concerned with where I was spending my days or what I was doing. I look back at my four years at Monte Vista much like I'm sure an ex-con looks at prison, i.e., I got through it and I got out.

While my friends were preparing to go off to college, I sat tight in my little box-like life, expecting that I'd live at home and go to the nearest junior college. Susan was finishing her last year at UCLA and my mom declared that at this time there wasn't enough money for both of us to live away from home while attending college. My parents had never encouraged me to make something of myself. I think my mom somehow figured in her warped way that because I placed pressure on myself to do well, she never had to offer support and encouragement. I can't recall her ever asking what I wanted to do with the rest of my life or suggesting I could be this or that, that I was smart enough or good enough to carve out a good life for myself.

Most people want a better life for their kids than they had, but I never got that sense from my parents. As a result, I didn't expend too much energy focusing on either career or educational opportunities. To me, a junior college was like an extension of high school. I knew I was fairly smart, but I lacked the confidence and parental support to overcome this and all my other insecurities. I'd been struggling with bulimia for nearly five years and that was the one area of my life that could demand my undivided attention. I was careful whenever my girlfriends talked about what colleges they applied for and how they heard back from this one or that one. I avoided engaging in such conversations, fearful they might ask me questions I'd be embarrassed to answer. Why aren't you going away? Don't you want to? Can't you afford it? Secretly I was heartbroken that I wasn't even applying to colleges like all my friends, even just to see if I'd be accepted.

But knowing that I couldn't afford to pay for tuition, fees, housing, and such myself, I turned my feelings inward and numbed myself through my bulimia. For now I would settle for the numbing effect of food and binging and purging to help me overpower my sadness or disappointment.

During the summer of 1986 I was about to fill out my class schedule for Diablo Valley College, the junior college Susan had attended, when without any explanation my mother said, "Jocelyn, you can apply to college if you like. You can live away from home to go to school, like your friends." I think it was Susan who convinced her. Susan was very intelligent, very persuasive, and loved the entire experience she was having at UCLA. I think she somehow knew I was disappointed living at home and going to the local junior college. Because it was already the beginning of July when I got the news, I now worried it was too late to be accepted anywhere. Everyone I knew had received their acceptance letters before graduation. Susan stepped in and helped me again. She was tenacious, calling several different colleges, asking which majors were still open. Eventually she found that Cal Poly in San Luis Obispo had an opening in their Natural Resources Department. She and I, but mostly Susan, filled out the application requesting admission to their Natural Resources Department, i.e., digging in the dirt but I didn't care. The dirt in San Luis Obispo seemed quite appealing at this point. The envelope from Cal Poly arrived several weeks later. I was accepted. Soon I'd be living away from home. How grateful I was at that moment to Susan.

I loved that Cal Poly was a good four-hour drive away from my home. The farther away the better, I thought. Also, Cal Poly was smaller than many colleges, more like a private college and that seemed better suited to me because I was so shy and timid. After receiving my letter of acceptance, I had only three weeks before I'd actually be living on campus. I wouldn't be attending classes my first week. The college offered what they called WOW week or The Week of Welcome, when a week of events introduces the entire freshman class to the campus, facilities, town, etc. I was eager to attend and live away from home and excited to finally call my own shots. Now I would no longer feel that every part of my private life was being invaded. My mom could no longer snoop through my personal belongings, listen to my phone conversations, or lecture me about this or that being a sin rather than involving herself in my life in a positive way.

My excitement and eagerness began to wane as the reality of my situation sunk in. What had seemed like the best opportunity in my life to date was eclipsed by fear and trepidation. What was I thinking? I was bulimic. For the very first time I was confronted with the possibility of having others discover my secret. Panic gripped me, and the fear that I would not be able to cope with the dual pressures of college and bulimia overwhelmed me. What if my dorm mates discovered I was obsessed with food? What would they think of me? What was I to do?

I decided the time had come for me to confront my mom with the truth about my illness. I had to tell her I was bulimic, that I had been so since the first month of eighth grade. Desperate for some support, direction, and help, I approached her in the afternoon while she was doing laundry and told her of my situation. Her reaction was nothing like I expected or hoped for. "Mom I have something very important to tell you. I don't know how exactly to say it so I will just say it like it is. I'm bulimic. I've been bulimic since the eighth grade, two weeks before my thirteenth birthday to be exact."

I watched my mother from behind as she walked up the stairs with clean clothes in her arms. She stopped suddenly, turned around, and stared at me. What was she thinking? I couldn't read her mind, let alone tell anything from her body language. But immediately after that fleeting thought, the color drained from her face and she looked as if she'd seen a ghost. She seemed overcome for a moment. Was she going to reach out to me? Would she care? She clearly always had her suspicions. I was nervous, yet hopeful too. Little beads of sweat began to appear on my nose and forehead. After a few moments of silence, she began to cry hysterically. I thought at first she was crying for me, but I was mistaken. I soon discovered she was crying for herself.

I felt attacked and abandoned as she told me that what I'd just confessed hurt her enormously. "How could you do this to me? Can't you just stop?" she cried. I sensed she was appalled or angered by the revelation. Somehow my severe problem became a problem not about me but about her. She wasn't acting like a concerned parent. Otherwise I wouldn't be staring at her hurt and angry face and wishing that maybe I'd never said anything. Instead of trying to parent, comfort, and support me, she basically proceeded to make me feel guilty for even telling her. She acted like she didn't know I'd been throwing up for years, ignoring the fact she constantly tapped on the bathroom door, yelled at me to quit eating, and even smelled my hands when I exited the bathroom. "Why can't you just eat less? I do and I'm thin."

I thought my confession had caused her pain and anguish, and that, in turn, made me feel guiltier for telling her. I didn't know at the time that we bulimics feel guilty about everything. I wished right then I'd never bothered to tell her. It was a total misjudgment on my part to think she would actually want to help me with my battle and not twist it into her problem, as she had always done, not just with me but also with my sisters and my dad. She would appropriate everything that happened and turn it into her problem. She reacted to every situation by telling everyone what an effect it had on her, even when it was obvious others were suffering. My heart plummeted to the pit of my stomach. I knew right then, based on her selfish reaction I wasn't going to get any help from her. Instead, she proceeded for the next fifteen minutes or so to tell me how devastated she was and how I'd just hurt her more than anyone before.

During my mother's diatribe, she never referenced me or my eating disorder. She never said to me, "Jocelyn, I will do anything it takes to help you. We will work this out," or, "Jocelyn I will find out what we need to do and who we need to see to get you better." It was me who consoled her tears, telling her I'd be okay, that I could deal with this. She cruelly dismissed the deep longing I had for her to show a level of selflessness by attempting to help me, even consult with a doctor on my behalf. She chose to get upset and act as if my being bulimic was somehow hurting her more than it was me. What was she thinking? How could she take someone else's severe illness and turn it on herself? That was crazy. I can't even to this day understand that way of thinking. After she stopped her uncontrolled sobbing and ranting about how much I'd just upset her, she proceeded to try and convince me that if I made a big enough effort, I could simply control my addiction to food. Her parting words of wisdom, which were the furthest thing from that, were, "Jocelyn, just don't overeat. If you do this, then you won't get fat and feel the need to throw up."

It was that simple to her. Don't eat a lot and you won't feel the urge to throw up. Wow, how come I hadn't thought of that? What a great suggestion. She obviously had zero comprehension or even will to understand what I had told her, I wanted to scream at her, "I am bulimic. I can't control what I eat and do not eat. That's my problem. My problem can't be solved by telling me to stop eating like a pig so I won't feel guilty and feel the need to throw up."

At that point, it no longer mattered, I had to leave. I couldn't survive in that house any longer. There was nothing left for me. Growing up in my family was far from happy to begin with and this was the final straw. She cut off any further discussion by saying, "This is your one chance to go to college, and you don't want to blow it just because you are bulimic."

My fate for the next eighteen years was sealed that day on the stairway. The past few years were just the beginning of my long battle with bulimia. I would spend my young adult life all the way into my thirties living with the disease day and night. The ensuing years would be filled with unimaginable consequences. The tricks I learned, the lies I told to keep the disorder hidden, and the sacrifices I made are ones I wish with all my heart that nobody else will ever experience. My lifestyle wasn't something I willingly chose. I tumbled headlong into it, not knowing where it would lead. Bulimia became the means for me to survive, as ugly and grotesque as it is. Strange as it may sound, I needed bulimia, with all of its destructiveness. Otherwise, it's possible I would not be here today.

Chapter 11

Backwards into Hell

I had mixed feelings about living outside my comfort zone, but I hoped going to Cal Poly would bring about a new and better chapter in my life. With only three weeks to get ready, I couldn't focus on how exciting college would be, meeting new people, hanging out, having fun. All I could think of was what I would do in terms of my bulimia. I knew that hiding binging and purging would be far more difficult to accomplish than I had experienced before because I was going to live in the dorms. I would not only share a room with someone there, but also I would share a bathroom with all the girls on the dorm floor. I had survived on eating little to nothing before, even though it made me sick and decided I would have to put my energy into following this regimen rather than eating and throwing up. I figured no one would suspect me of being bulimic if I restricted my food intake. In a perverse way, I took my mom's advice. "Jocelyn, just don't overeat and you won't need to throw up." I committed to swapping bulimia for anorexia, at least for a time, as it would be far less noticeable and subject to ridicule.

Neither my dad nor my mom offered to accompany me on the drive to Cal Poly, which was a relief. I drove myself, in my dad's old, brown Oldsmobile Omega, listening to the songs playing on the radio while the miles flew by. It had finally happened, I was leaving home. I drove along the freeway, filled with happiness and excited about being on a large college campus surrounded by thousands and thousands of students, with no family or town of Alamo to watch and comment on my every action. For the first time in recent memory, I felt contentment fill my heart. I believed living in this place might allow me to be noticed for me and not for all the perceptions and baggage I labored under back home.

After I settled into my dorm room, I was convinced this was the best thing that had happened for me. Despite my concerns about being able to stop my bulimia, the overwhelming sense of happiness that I was finally far enough away from where I spent my formative years inspired me to make some changes. I was committed to losing even more weight now. Being at college was

89

going to be different I told myself, so I needed to do whatever it took to make this the best situation possible. With this renewed commitment I managed to lose another ten pounds in just a few short weeks and got down to one hundred twenty-two pounds. How wonderful I felt and how pleased at losing weight on my own terms, no weekly weigh-ins, no funny looks from the diet counselors or disappointed stares from my mom. It was a complete relief to not have to go to some crazy, embarrassing center to lose weight. I was determined to do it on my own, without anyone's help and without the peer pressure I felt at Monte Vista High. I had complete freedom to choose what I would and would not eat. How liberated I felt.

After I lost my first ten pounds at college, I noticed that, again, I was receiving more attention. Guys and girls, ones I knew and ones I didn't, seemed to show some level of interest in me as my frame shrunk. I never had a strong personality while growing up, so I found even this little bit of attention strangely pleasurable. Deep inside, I realized I wasn't going to make a lot of friends. My eating disorder prevented me from getting too close to anyone, but I certainly enjoyed being regarded as a person and not just as some anonymous fat kid. Still, with a little nervousness, I allowed myself to feel what I perceived as the empowerment and opportunities that being thin provided. I was determined and fixated on losing still more weight.

Freshman year I had only one real girlfriend, Susie. She, too, had attended Monte Vista High and we'd been pretty friendly throughout those four years. Because Susie and I had a history, it was easy for us to pick up where we left off and build a deeper friendship. Eventually we became roommates and, from that moment, we did practically everything together. We'd study, go to parties, go to the beach, and laugh together. I was having a great time hanging out with her. She and I became as close as I could be to someone. Besides being good friends, I admired Susie from a physical standpoint. She had a great figure and for as long as I can remember, she was never a big eater. Susie ate only enough to satisfy her appetite and not because she needed to fill some inner void. Because she ate unlike anyone I knew—what normal eating is, I believe—my strange eating habits and attitude to food didn't prompt her to interrogate me. She never probed as to why I didn't use my meal card and join her for dinner in the canteen with everyone else. I was relieved she chose not to ask me questions and concluded she figured I was dieting and didn't want to pry. I weighed more than she did and had already told her I was trying to lose a few pounds. I was grateful she respected my silence, as restriction was certainly working for me and that was all I needed.

There were quite a few different cafeterias on campus offering every type of food imaginable. I accepted the fact these were places I could lose control and eat everything in sight. My bulimia was so powerful that once a trigger food such as bread, crackers, or pretzels, sugary foods such as pastries, cookies, candy, ice cream, or high-calorie foods such as fries, burgers, cheese, etc. hit the back of my throat, there was no turning back. The world would disappear, and I would be in a bulimic haze, unable to stop myself until the urge to eat was gone. To avoid making a spectacle of myself, I stayed away from the cafeterias as much as possible. Particularly at night, I chose not to go because it was much harder for me to control my urges. To this day, daytime isn't as difficult for me—my therapist and I call the evening my "witching hour," when my demons come to visit in force. By not going to one of the many cafeterias as everyone I knew did, I was able to avoid temptation and the seductive lure of all the delicious foods or even feel the pressure of the hunger pangs as my body cried out for nourishment. I preferred to go hungry than be caught in a crazy food binge in public.

When all my neighbors and Susie headed to the dining hall for dinner, I'd go to the gym instead and take an hour-long class of high-impact aerobics. I had signed up for a year's membership at Calendar Girls, a women-only gym, where I wouldn't have to worry about my fat wiggling and jiggling all over in front of men as I sweated like a mad woman on the aerobic floor—women are a little more forgiving. Calendar Girls suited me perfectly. By doing a little research, I discovered my aerobic class burned anywhere from three hundred fifty to four hundred fifty calories. What a great substitute for binging and purging. I calculated that by walking around campus during the day and ending with an aerobics class, I could burn all the calories I had allowed myself to eat during the day. Because I couldn't deny my intense hunger pangs after my workout, I felt safe allowing myself around two hundred calories, figuring I'd sleep that off during the night. I'd have a cup or two of air-popped popcorn, plain or sometimes with low-calorie, powdered butter substitute, and a mug of fat-free hot cocoa. Closing my eyes as I tried to go to sleep, I'd calculate every single bite of food I'd ingested and conclude I was eating about seven hundred calories a day. Happy in that knowledge, I could sleep soundly.

Every once in a while Susie would pressure me to join her for dinner. "Jocelyn, please come to the cafeteria with me. You haven't come with me in such a long time. Come on, be my company just for tonight. Skip aerobics class, it won't kill you." So during one of my very infrequent visits to the cafeteria, I tried my best to ignore all the food surrounding me. Hamburgers sizzled on the stove, French fries cooked in oil, ready-made tacos displayed in rows just called out to me, and cookies, my greatest temptation, lay everywhere.

I somehow managed to avoid the sights and smells of the very wonderful and delicious-looking foods and occupied myself people watching. One of those times, my eyes came to rest on a guy who looked nothing like the boys I knew or grew up around. He looked like a surfer-skater with long, bleached-out hair and a pierced ear, and he wore one of the most outrageous outfits I'd seen on campus so far, a ripped T-shirt and jeans that had hand-painted skulls, scary faces, and weird designs all over them. I was instantly attracted to him. His individualism appealed to me. With my attention so completely diverted elsewhere, I couldn't be bothered with eating, a rarity for me. I managed to only pick at my food. Susie couldn't help but notice I was staring at him. Much bolder than me, she went right up to him and began to talk. Within minutes, she escorted him to our table. We were introduced and within that very week, Matt became my first real boyfriend.

Before meeting Matt, I had taken off several more pounds. I was fluctuating between one hundred seventeen and one hundred nineteen pounds, and even that was significant for me. Since high school, I had grown two inches and was now five feet five inches tall. I knew that was to my advantage in terms of weight. I went from wearing a size eight to a size six and I was delighted to give my size eights to the Salvation Army.

Whenever I lost weight, I took another step towards becoming a more confident person. The scale continued to dictate how I felt about myself and my ability to interact with the world at large. But even as I lost weight and began to have people like Matt interested in me, I couldn't help questioning the genuineness of it all. Would they have liked me or even given me the time of day if they had seen me back in high school? I didn't think so. The euphoria losing weight provided simply reinforced my need to become even slimmer. I now set my sights on wearing a size four instead of a six. I was completely convinced that because I was no longer fat and Matt liked me as he saw me today, he would like me even more if I was thinner. I continued my quest, convinced that being thin was the only way to ensure that people took an interest in me. I resolved to continue restricting my diet to the specific foods I felt safe with, and I'd work out even harder at Calendar Girls every day at dinner time. I was not going to risk jeopardizing my journey to the magical world of the thin people.

As Matt and I spent more time together, I discovered, unlike all the other college guys I had met to date, he wasn't a big drinker. This new information was great, because I certainly hated feeling the pressure to drink more than one or two light beers. Beer was linked to overwhelming negative emotions that prompted a frantic dialog in my head. Jocelyn, I'd think, you are going to blow up like a big fat balloon drinking all that beer. Jocelyn, you are going to look just like you did back in high school. Jocelyn, no one will like you, not even Matt, if you get fat. Remember those infamous words your mother always said, "Jocelyn, if you'd only lose weight then you'd be happy." On those rare occasions when I gave in and indulged in excess drinking, the following days would be difficult for me. My head would spin, my heart would race, and I would be stricken with guilt over the beer calories I had consumed. I equated drinking to calories, not to having a good time and enjoying myself as others would. Drinking was adding forbidden calories to my diet, and calories in the form of liquid rather than food didn't seem a good trade to me. If I wanted more calories, I certainly wanted them in the form of food. I liked the excitement of going to a party, so when we'd drink, I'd alter my day's food plan. I'd add the alcohol calories I'd consumed into my daily allotment. This meant I'd mentally prepare myself all day for the evening's drinking. I'd try everything I could to convince myself that should I have a few beers, I wouldn't get fat and be like I was back in Alamo. But besides using self-talk all day long, I had to have other contingencies. I'd cut back on my food intake for the day and allow myself to eat only one bagel and eight malt balls, nothing else. If I did this, then I felt reassured I wouldn't metamorphose overnight into the huge, ugly person I believed I once was. Even with this strict regimen, I still felt overwhelming guilt afterwards. It mattered little to me that I more or less starved myself all day, ignoring the intense jabbing pains in my torso caused by the ever-tightening knots in my stomach as my hunger grew—all this work just to have a few beers and appear normal to the rest of the girls at the party. The morning, when others slept off their hangovers, I would work out harder than usual. I'd take two aerobic classes and walk for two hours.

As my freshman year drew to an end, so too did my relationship with Susie. We had gotten to know one another's personalities, and with that came the realization we were very different people. We slowly grew apart. Personality differences aside, our friendship dynamics changed one upsetting Friday afternoon. Without warning and for no reason other than, I believe, spite, Susie had a meeting with our Residents' Assistant (RA), the "student babysitter" who oversaw the dorm floor. During her meeting with Kathy, Susie told her I was bulimic. Living together, it was impossible for Susie not to realize that I had more serious issues surrounding food beyond just a desire to be trim. It was pretty obvious, since I went to the cafeteria for dinner only a handful of times, ate popcorn at night instead of real food, and constantly worked out. Armed with her suspicions, Susie decided to act, I believe, out of spite rather than concern. I think she became jealous when I began to weigh less than she did, as she had begun to put on a few extra pounds and resented my laser focus on a weight loss program. So she revealed my deepest, darkest secret, the demon that existed in the furthest recesses of my being, to Kathy. I was beyond devastated when Kathy asked to speak with me in private and relayed her conversation with Susie. Apparently someone had been heard throwing up in the dorm bathroom and Kathy said based on her conversation with Susie, she believed it was me.

I was totally thrown off balance. I had worked hard to keep my disease hidden from my dorm mates. I never binged and purged in the shared bathrooms or anywhere within the dorm. I swore to Kathy it was not me who was bulimic. It couldn't be, I told her, as I didn't indulge. Even Kathy knew I went to Calendar Girls every night to work out instead of eating in the cafeteria like all the other girls. Finally after a long and drawn out conversation, I managed to convince Kathy it wasn't me who was throwing up in the bathroom.

What prompted me to believe that Susie had nothing but ill intentions toward me was the well-known fact that another girl in our dorm, Karen, struggled with bulimia. Luckily for me, one of those moments occurred that reestablishes a person's faith in people. Karen saw how devastated I was and that others were shunning me. Nobody spoke to me anymore so I more or less remained in my room if I wasn't in classes or with Matt. She admitted to the RA and the girls in our dorm that it was she who had bulimia and not me.

As courageous as Karen was and as thankful as I was, it did little to change the other girls' perception. My reputation was tarnished and despite Karen's confession, the girls remained distant. I became increasingly more dependent on Matt, which simply increased the distance between me and the rest of the dorm.

There was no way Matt didn't know I had "real problems" with food, but he chose not to broach the subject and never asked a single question about the whole bulimia incident, which had inevitably spread to the adjacent dorms, including his. I thought maybe it was because he was embarrassed by the rumors surrounding me so he thought it best not to ask any questions. Or maybe he didn't want to get involved. I'll never know. Though I was disappointed he didn't seem concerned enough to reach out to me, I was also relieved not to have to try and explain myself either, my usual catch-22. It was hard enough trying to cover up my obsessive-compulsive behaviors. I believed I had so many issues and so little to offer to him that I worried constantly he would dump me. For that reason, I preferred not to discuss my eating with him. I decided I'd rather have him around, support or no support, than lose him and be alone.

No matter what I was doing, attending class, studying, or trying to have fun with Matt, I was haunted by my ever-present thoughts about my weight. Jocelyn your stomach is protruding. Jocelyn your inner thighs seem closer together than yesterday. Jocelyn your face looks extremely bloated, you are retaining water, I'd chastise myself. I'd always try to calculate every single calorie I ate. Was the malted milk ball bigger than the rest and if so, did it have more calories? How many might that be? Did I intentionally pick the larger bagel knowing I could have only one? Did I put too much non-dairy creamer in my coffee? Aside from the negative self-talk, I'd also contemplate how many calories I'd burn while exercising if I did just aerobics or if I wore my wrist weights because they increased my heart rate and that meant burning extra calories. The most important question I'd ask myself, though, was how much will I weigh when I step onto the scale? As compulsive as I was about every bit of food I ate, how many calories this exercise or that exercise would burn, and calculating how many hours I could stand versus sitting, I dared weigh myself only on safe days, days I didn't feel like I was extra fat or retaining fluid.

One afternoon, feeling particularly safe, I decided to weigh myself. As I made sure no one was standing too near to me, I stepped onto the cold, grey scale at Calendar Girls. First, I lifted my right leg then my left so as not to jolt the scale and cause an inaccurate reading. With fear filling every fiber, I slowly moved the weight bar to the right, pound by pound. One hundred pounds. Too much. The bar sank to the bottom. I couldn't believe it. I cautiously slid the bar to the left, ever so slightly. Ninety-eight pounds, ninety-seven pounds, and finally, I stopped at ninety-six, the bar balancing in the middle. I weighed ninety-six pounds. I gasped quietly. Five feet five inches tall and I weighed ninety-six pounds. I was overwhelmed with happiness. For the first time ever, I felt as though I was truly thin, and not fat. In my mind, I wasn't too thin, I could never be. Rather I was not fat and that's what mattered. I weighed less than a hundred pounds. I couldn't be that fat kid anymore if that's what the scale said I weighed. Filled with an indescribable joy, I left the gym and almost skipped home to my dorm room. Pretty much anorexic, I was finally happy!

Fortunately, I managed to maintain decent grades despite my real focus being on my twenty-four-hour-a-day weight battle. I rarely missed attending my classes and always did whatever work was required. I even managed to go out every weekend. But school and the weekends meant little to me. Inside I was falling apart, and I knew this. My out-of-control addiction was ruling every thought and action in my life. This deep, dark path led me to indulge in larger quantities of diet and water pills—five, six, sometimes seven a day—and using laxatives more frequently, if not once a day than at least once every other day. I was exhausted physically and emotionally, but I couldn't seem to stop the downward spiral. I had no one to talk to and never dared to speak to Matt about my real problems. I worried too much about pleasing him and being the loving and kind girlfriend. Should I divulge my most horrific secret, I figured I'd lose him and end up having absolutely no one in my life. It was just not worth the risk, and because he knew something wasn't right and chose to ignore it, I left it at that.

As finals arrived and the year drew to an end, my hunger pangs grew and I began to fantasize about embarking on my old binge drive-bys. I missed eating real food, tasting crunchy and sugary cereal and toast or even a Weight Watchers frozen entrée. I missed the sensation of cold ice cream and yogurt as they glided down my throat. I missed eating food, period. I had restricted for so long, I was exhausted. The mental energy and willpower it required was draining from me, and I was growing weaker and weaker. On the flip side, I knew I was incapable of controlling how much I'd eat if I didn't stick to the restrictive diet I was on. Even fantasizing about eating caused great anguish in me. Guilt feelings emerged. Self-doubt and fears of losing whatever level of control I believed I had finally achieved engulfed me and left me in endless inner turmoil. The funny thing in a way was that these were fantasies—I never savored something bite by bite or let food glide down my throat. When binging, I would eat in a crazed manner, shoving down as much food as possible in the shortest time. I never tasted it, and rarely caught the faintest aroma. I ate in a fast, efficient manner to binge and purge. Still, my thoughts of food became stronger each day.

I couldn't afford to stay down south and had no choice but to return home for summer break. The thought of going to Alamo brought all the old feelings and fears to the surface. Could I continue to restrict? I didn't think so. In a strange sort of way, I twisted my not wanting to live at home into something I looked forward to—I would have the privacy and opportunity to binge and purge. I could be delivered from this hell of eternal hunger for a few short months. I could return to comforting myself with my dear, old friend, food.

Chapter 12

Home Sweet Hurt

It was the summer of 1987. I was eighteen, driving north along Highway 101, heading back to that dark, dreary house and bedroom that I would pretend was home for the next three months. Was I going to visit all my old haunts, Burger King, Taco Bell, and Yogurt Castle? Or was I going to be able to control my cravings and continue to restrict? I doubted it, and my body seemed to be pushing me to get home as quickly as possible. It was like my demon, and not me, was driving the car. I raced past King City, a place notorious for giving speeding tickets even at a mere two miles over the speed limit, and the farmland, oblivious to everything except the road that lay ahead of me, the physical one I was on and the mental one I had to navigate during the coming months. *Am I making a mistake by going home?* The real me knew the answer but the bulimic me just lied and said everything would be fine. It didn't matter, though, because I had no choice. I had no money saved. I didn't see how I could afford to pay rent, let alone all my other living expenses. I had to go home for a while and get a full-time job. This would be a tough summer.

I paused in front of the big, brown wooden door of my parents' house. Hardly a second had passed before I was consumed by the same feelings I had in high school. Without any warning, I was once again the fat, insecure, unworthy, and timid teenager. None of the freedom I had felt while living at Cal Poly had survived the journey home.

"Hi, Mom," I said as I walked through the front door.

"Hi, Jocelyn." As usual, my mom was sitting in the living room in her favorite cream-colored chair, waiting for my arrival. We hugged and she looked at me but never said anything about my weight. She had seen me a few times in the intervening months when I made quick weekend trips home for necessities, but she never brought up the additional weight I'd lost or how she thought I looked at ninety-six pounds. I guess I was thin enough that my weight was now a non-issue.

As we embraced, the only thing I could concentrate on was finding out what foods she had in the kitchen. I cared little about talking with her and telling her about my journey home, let alone school, so as soon as I dropped my bags in the entry way, I walked straight to the kitchen to see what foods were hiding in the cupboards and refrigerator. "Mom, I haven't eaten all day," I professed, a lie, of course. I tried to disguise as best I could the fact I wasn't physically, but emotionally, hungry. I needed a rapid intake of food to fill the void inside me that seemed to have reawakened with a vengeance during our obligatory hug. I made a frozen dinner, had a couple slices of bread slathered in butter, ate handfuls of crackers, and poured myself a glass of juice. Then like always, I told her I had a stomachache and needed to use the bathroom. The house was the same, my mom was the same, and I felt the same as I had during all the time that I had lived on dreary Austin Lane. I forgot what it felt like to feel differently. The Cal Poly me had vanished. I could not escape the shadow of the fat me that seemed to lurk just out of view, calling to me, mocking me. "You thought you could run away and hide but you can't...."

I went to the bathroom, took out the blue throw-up can, placed it in the center of the toilet seat, and threw up everything I'd just eaten. I felt exceptionally faint after as I hadn't purged like this in so long. It literally knocked the wind out of me. With sweat pouring down my face and back, I laid on the cold tile floor until I began to recover. Only when I was able to look in the mirror to see the color creep back into my face did I dare leave the dark, ugly bathroom. Now I can deal with the rest of the afternoon, I told myself. I was numb and nothing could affect me for a time.

Each day that whole summer while living at home I engaged in some of my most horrific and violent bulimic episodes. For some reason I could now eat more in one sitting than I ever could before. It was as if I had the capacity of two large men. Everyday I embarked on one of my drive-by binges, going to Burger King, then Taco Bell, McDonald's, Yogurt Castle, and finally, 7-Eleven just for the sake of eating a little more. As usual, I drove home like a maniac, speeding, running red lights, and not concentrating on the road or other drivers. My mission was to get home right away, head straight to the bathroom, run a pretend bath to try and mask the noise, and throw up the whole afternoon's calories.

It didn't take long to land a full-time cashier's job at Copeland's Sporting Goods in Walnut Creek. It was a pretty good job for me because there was no temptation in the way there was flipping hotdogs at the greasy spoon. The bad news was Copeland's was conveniently located close to all my favorite drive-by binge places. No matter what shift I worked, there was always the opportunity for some serious restaurant hopping. No one at work would see me eating because I never ate in front of anyone except Matt or sometimes, though not by choice, my mom. I was pretty sure I could easily hide my bulimia from my coworkers. I'd always wait until after work to eat, and then I'd rampage through each eatery in turn, not stopping until I could eat no more. I worked five days a week making minimum wage, five dollars fifty cents per hour. I tried to save some money for the following school year's living expenses but it all went on food.

I was now back in a familiar mode, out of control, binging and purging multiple times a day. Everything in my life seemed to be beyond my influence. I couldn't stop eating everything in sight, I couldn't avoid living in my parent's house, even if it was only for three months, and I could barely concentrate enough to make it through the workday. I was falling deeper and deeper into the clutches of my disease. With my descent, my abuse of all varieties of over-the-counter pills grew. Diet pills, water pills, and laxatives—I had fallen prey to their false promises. I became dependent on them and convinced myself everyday that maybe today would be the day that the pills would finally work their magic. I took one after the other, usually ingesting upwards of ten of each. There was no magic, but even so, I couldn't stop taking them. At the time I didn't know the permanent and irreparable damage they were doing to me and the consequences I'd suffer because of them. Even today, as I stroll through the aisles of a drugstore, I can't help thinking of the potential harm these OTC products can cause if abused. Yet there are no controls over who can buy them and in what quantities.

As the summer wore on, my weight increased apace. No longer restricting, but eating everything I could meant I was putting on the pounds rapidly. Even throwing up, it was impossible to eliminate everything. No longer did I weigh ninety-six. Five pounds, ten pounds, fifteen pounds came piling on in what seemed like the blink of any eye.

With the increase in weight came the renewed sense of worthlessness followed by deeper withdrawal into myself. I felt sick and fatigued all the time. The summer was one big blur. I had managed to defeat myself once again. I had failed miserably in controlling my eating and maintaining my Cal Poly weight. Most of all, I had failed because my illusions of a better life that college had promised had disintegrated and in its wake I was more bulimic than ever. I was now far worse emotionally and physically than I had ever been. I felt I had reached the point of no return.

When I left Alamo, I waved goodbye to my mom and hoped it would be a very long time before I'd have to visit again. I hated that summer and was happy just knowing that a whole year of school lay ahead of me. I had saved little money while working at the sporting goods store, but I felt fortunate because I could easily transfer working at the Walnut Creek location to their San Luis Obispo store. I liked this idea much better than having to try and sell myself to someone else just to get another crummy cashier's position. With finding a job out of the way, I could concentrate on how I would live with my disease.

That year, rather than the dorm, I was going to live with two guys and a girl in a lovely, two-story town home just down the street from the dorm I had lived in the previous year. It was only a few years old, so it had the modern conveniences and some extras, such as laundry facilities and a large swimming pool that our kitchen overlooked. I was glad to be living in such a nice place, but the big question was, what was I going to do about my eating? Would I restrict like I did while in the dorms? Or would I binge and purge like I had all summer? The dilemma distressed me. I just didn't have the answer. I didn't know if I had the same level of willpower that I'd possessed the previous year. My physical need was intense. I would shake and sweat with anxious anticipation before a binge. Bulimia was my only means to satisfy this and my emotional cravings. My closest companion, my bulimic me, drew me in. I couldn't resist, so I extinguished all thoughts of restricting and focused on how I would hide my bulimia from my roommates.

There was no missing I'd gained weight, nearly twenty pounds, over the summer. I felt it across my whole body and deep inside my brain. I decided the best way to readdress losing weight was to carefully monitor my binges and to exercise more. While watching what foods I binged and purged—certain foods like ice cream and cereal are much easier to eliminate than foods like peanut butter—I took advantage of the fifty-meter swimming pool on campus. Every morning at five, I'd wake, drink two cups of coffee, pop a caffeine pill in my mouth, and head off to the pool. There I'd swim non-stop for an hour straight, calculating I'd burn roughly four hundred calories, what I considered a very good way to start off my day. After classes were over and I'd completed my shift at work, I'd head to Calendar Girls to do an hour of high-impact aerobics, just like I did freshman year. Little by little, I could see my hard work and total dedication pay off. I was shedding some weight, not a lot, but any loss helped control the worse excesses of my emotions.

As the months passed, I cared less and less about school, making friends, or much of anything else other than my obsession with bulimia and spending time with Matt. I resumed engaging in my usual binge drive-bys. Burgers, French fries, and numerous candy bars, I'd gobble down as quickly and fanatically as I could. I'd sip soda in between to help my purge not be so tough on my esophagus, which any continual abuser can verify could hurt like hell. Then I'd drive like a maniac, racing my digestive system to get home in time to run up the stairs and purge before any of those calories took root. Ultimately my binges couldn't be restricted to my drive-bys or whatever food I bought at the grocery store. I soon found I couldn't resist the temptation to steal food from my roommates. They ate like most college students with lots of junk food in their respective cupboards. What I thought of as bulimic innocence, taking a piece of their food here and there, rapidly became much more. Soon I wasn't able to stop at just stealing the odd cookie or bit of candy. I began to steal anything that was there such as bags of chocolate chip cookies and crackers, and devour them all, caring little for the consequence or for the fact that my roommates had spent their hard earned cash on them. I would be so engrossed in consuming their foods that I wouldn't even notice how much I was eating until it was too late. I tried my best to replace the food I stole, but I wasn't always able to and soon suspicion began to grow in the apartment about the increasing amounts of vanishing edibles. Small arguments erupted, usually the guys blaming each other, but nothing was ever resolved and no wonder, seeing it was me.

Although I managed to avoid suspicion, the atmosphere in the place soured. I knew my disease was bad now, especially because I had reached a different level, stealing to binge. I felt guilty and totally ashamed and couldn't admit to my roommates that it was me stealing food. I couldn't admit I had bulimia. I simply resolved to try and stop the stealing, but to no avail.

I fell into a state of complete oblivion, unable to relate to anyone, including Matt. I was deep in the throes of my disease. We hung out together but, not surprisingly, never had deep or meaningful conversations. He had problems of his own he'd brought into our relationship.

Matt was an only child, the son of very young parents. His mom was eighteen, his dad twenty when he was born. When Matt was two, his father walked out, leaving his mom to care for him alone until his grandparents stepped in to help raise him. Matt had always secretly yearned for a father and this intense yearning followed him into adulthood. He also experienced some severe trauma as a young child that fed his insecurities.

Matt's classmates teased him because he didn't have all the material things they did. His mother worked around the clock and, as a child, Matt was basically a loner. Not into scholastics, he found solace in skateboarding and surfing. When he was twelve, his mother remarried, but her new husband didn't care for Matt and it was apparent he couldn't wait for him to turn eighteen and leave home. Instead of defending Matt, his mother accepted the situation so as not to jeopardize her relationship with her new husband. When Matt turned eighteen, they sent him away with no money and left him to fend for himself.

He turned to drugs as a way of masking his authentic self and overcoming his feelings. This quickly disintegrated from recreational use and became a lifestyle which was quite apparent even during his first year in college. Later Matt skipped from job to job and lied to everyone to avoid any pain he felt the truth might bring. He also avoided any real level of responsibility. He told people what he thought they wanted to hear, unless he was backed into a corner when caught in one of his many lies.

Without much money or parental influence, Matt gradually became more self-centered and grabbed everything he could in an attempt to fill a void he refused to admit he had. Ironically, he had to be surrounded by people at all times, probably because he was alone so much of his childhood. I believe he loved me as best he could, given his inability to be emotionally intimate. My fundamental insecurities fed his and we became a codependent team or co-enablers. We sustained each other.

He needed me for comfort, but in reality could not give anything in return. When he was twenty-two, we found out his real father had apparently committed suicide—he was found dead in a canyon. This was a pivotal moment for him—the hope of his real dad returning to him was gone forever. He went steadily downhill from there. I was so messed up, I hung in, convinced there was something in it for me, but I just grew closer to my bulimic self. It was the only way I knew to cope with the intense loneliness and isolation I felt.

My world was slowly collapsing and the only way I could find any solace was either by a food or an exercise binge. There was nothing in between these two states but a fog of anxiety that I couldn't shake. My binging and purging grew worse with larger amounts and more violent purges. I wasn't satisfied with the rush swimming and doing aerobics provided. I needed something more to fill my void, so I started mountain bike riding.

By late year I was beginning to tire and feel overly fatigued all the time. My hectic schedule of classes, work, working out, and seeing Matt as much as possible was taking a huge toll on me. Finally I couldn't handle the pressure of my life any longer. I called home. "Mom, it's me. I've been thinking. I'd like to come home for the last quarter," I blurted out, not thinking it through but desperate for any respite. "I'm feeling a little overwhelmed and think it would be best if I took a leave of absence just for the quarter. I'll still go to school, DVC, so I won't lose any credits."

Based on my experience during the summer, home should have been the last place I wanted to go, but bulimics have a strange, blindly optimistic streak that makes us feel things will be different the next time. It is often what condemns us to repeat the behaviors or re-create the environments that are most toxic for us. Something in my life had to change and home, I felt, was the only feasible option. I was completely engrossed in my bulimia and its co-conspirators—OTC pills, exercise, and restricting when not binging, which I was attempting again to help me avoid stealing my roommates' food. I loved Matt, but it was becoming too difficult to deal with life in general while trying to hide my battle. I was running as fast as I could and feeling like any moment I would collapse from exhaustion.

My mom was delighted to have me back. To her I was always, and remain so to this day, her vehicle to vent her life's frustrations. "Of course you can come home. I assume you can make it okay with Cal Poly? You can live here, go to school, and take the quarter off from work." That was it. The very next day I went to the admissions office and filled out the necessary paperwork. I was officially on leave of absence as soon as the quarter ended.

Later that evening as I reflected on my decision, still not certain if I was making one of the biggest mistakes in my life or if it would be just the right medicine, I couldn't deny that I knew without a doubt my mom wouldn't reject my request. Every time we talked on the phone she would complain to me how she was either feeling sick—so I always had to console her—or how she was so lonely and missed me. For as long as I could remember, she and my dad had never sat in the same room to have a conversation. Having someone in the house with her would be a welcome change.

As I parked my car in the driveway, I immediately regretted my decision. While bulimics have blind optimism at times, it never lasts more than a fleeting moment when reality bites. An overwhelming feeling of anxiety and sadness enveloped me. What I thought might be the best decision for me at this time, quickly changed. I knew I had made a huge mistake.

As I walked through the front door, my mom greeted me with a smile and a hug. She was happy to have me home, even for a short while. She was lonely and relied on me to make her feel she had some purpose in life, something she often shared with me, though I always found it a little perplexing considering she never got involved in my life. Even when I was a little girl, it seemed more like I was the parent and she the child. I constantly comforted her, listened to her recite her many ailments and depressions, and always, always tried to appease her.

She didn't bother to question why I wanted to come home. I presumed she was satisfied accepting what little I said on the phone back in San Luis Obispo. I found it strange I could always tell when something was wrong with her, but it was a one-way street. Not even now did she sense that maybe something was wrong with me or that I was severely distressed. Beyond that, I still harbored hope she'd ask me about my bulimia, since we had never spoken about it again after the incident on the stairs. As always, she didn't take note or hear my silent cries. Instead, the conversation revolved around her and had little to do with me.

I withdrew further from the outside world. My sole purpose during my stay at home was to binge and purge. Other than occasionally seeing one of my high school girlfriends who had returned home from college that semester and attended the same junior college, and seeing Matt on the occasional weekend, I hung out alone. My addiction to food became so overpowering during this time I binged and purged up to five times a day. I considered a three-binge day a good day and soon five became the rule rather than the exception. The amount of food I would consume in one sitting was reaching gargantuan proportions, totaling between seven and ten thousand calories. I was getting the rest I'd hoped for, but now I seemed to have moved to almost twenty-four-hour-a-day bulimic rituals. After classes at the junior college finished for the day, I'd hit the drive-in take-out windows of Burger King, Taco Bell, Jack in the Box, and make brief stops at Yogurt Castle, 7-Eleven, or Longs Drugs. I'd buy happy meals and combo meals, then eat like a maniac, shoving the greasy burgers and fries down my throat as fast as possible to the point of bursting, then home at top speed to throw up.

The six years I spent binging and purging was beginning to take its toll on my body. I constantly felt run down and was susceptible to colds, sinus infections, and the flu. One day, though, my body finally had enough. I had a high fever, my throat felt as if it was going to explode, and my chest hurt badly. I felt sicker than ever and when I went to the doctor, he informed me I had pneumonia and a collapsed lung. I was moved to the local hospital where I spent the next several days lying on a cold cot alone on the fourth floor, an IV in my left arm and monitors bleeping all around me. I knew very well how I ended up there. The intensity of my bulimia and pill abuse had increased tenfold compared to a few months ago, let alone the preceding years. I had placed too much stress on my body, but I never told the doctors the real reason I had gotten sick, and my mom didn't seem to make the connection either.

As I began to regain my strength in the hospital, an irrational panic struck me. How many calories were in an IV bag? I was having a couple pumped into me everyday. Oh, my God, I thought, am I worse off in here? Will I gain weight, while I can't work out? I didn't care that I had pneumonia and a collapsed lung. My focus was on the potential weight gain and the unhappiness that would bring. It was a measure of how warped bulimia had made my perspective that I could lie in a hospital worried only about the calorie content of an IV bag and not about my overall health.

After a four-day stay in John Muir, I returned home and was expected to be on bed rest. Instead of doing that, I headed to downtown Alamo to do a mini drive-by. I stopped at Safeway, the local donut shop, Thrifty drugstore, and 7-Eleven. When I returned, I pretended I was going to rest. I fetched the blue throw-up can from the upstairs bathroom and raced to my room. Since I was "resting," I was forced to use the small, half bath in my room, something I tried to avoid, due to the low water pressure in there. As I threw up, I felt such intense pain in my chest I had to cup my left rib with my hand to try and overcome the agony I felt with each purge. Although I worried I might pass out or do some damage to myself, it did little to stop me from continuing to get rid of the binge food. Along with the pain came blood and bile flowing out of my mouth and nose, but I kept on throwing up. I didn't care. I'd suffer through it and hope for the best. I had to get rid of the food.

Despite that incident, I went back to my daily multiple binge cycles and—no great surprise—I relapsed and had to return to John Muir. My lung collapsed again, only this time my vitals were better so I was given medicine and told to go home and stay in bed for several days. I followed the doctor's instructions and even stopped binging and purging for three days, practically a miracle at this stage of my disease. Once I was feeling better, off I went to Walnut Creek and all my favorite binge places.

I had more time at my disposal because I wasn't working. I exercised longer and harder than I had to date, usually three or more hours a day. Mornings and evenings I would run five miles and either go to the gym or do an hour and a half of aerobics by myself in my room while listening to music. I felt compelled to use my free time, thinking I should not only take advantage of purging, but working out too. I thought it would help in my battle to lose weight.

I began to weigh myself regularly, something I had once feared. First thing I did each morning as I stood naked with nothing in my stomach, not even a sip of water, was to step onto the scale and see what the bold black numbers said. If I weighed less than the day before, I was happy. If I weighed the same, I was frustrated and if I weighed more than the day before, even just a quarter of a pound, I was devastated. My day was ruined and, consequently, I would abuse more OTC pills than my usual allotment and binge and purge more times and with more violence. I could hear that nine-year-old child's voice calling me from the darkness of the past, telling me I was too fat, that if I wasn't losing weight every day or at a minimum maintaining, then I was a failure. I deserved to be punished.

When I returned to San Luis Obispo, I resolved never to go back to Alamo. Once again, I had regressed while there and instead of getting my act together, I did the opposite. I discovered a level of my disease beyond anything I had imagined. Driving back to San Luis, I felt calmer, though I worried about facing my roommates, who hadn't taken my leaving too well. Still I was more relieved to be on my own once more.

It was summer quarter and I opted not to take any classes. I'd work full time instead. I landed a job selling discount shoes in a strip mall where I was familiar with every inch because of my drive-bys. Following my nightmare three months at home, I found it impossible to rely on my willpower to help me stop binging and solely restrict. I knew this time I'd just have to be more careful. So I spent the entire summer of 1998 doing pretty much the same activities every day—working, secretly binging and purging, and hanging out with Matt.

One day I received a terribly disturbing phone call from my mom. "Jocelyn," she said in between her uncontrollable sobs, "I have breast cancer."

"What?" I couldn't believe what I was hearing. I was home less than a month ago and nothing seemed wrong with her then.

"The doctors found cancer in one of my breasts, and I need to have a mastectomy," she continued. "I'm going to have surgery in less than two weeks. I'm devastated," she mumbled through her sobs.

When I heard this traumatic news, I nearly dropped the phone. I started to cry, too, even though I tried my best to cover up my emotions. I didn't want to let her know how disturbing I thought this news was. She was more hysterical than I could remember her being since I was a child, and I didn't want to say anything that might upset her any more than she already was.

As soon as I could get my things organized, I headed back to Alamo, just a short time since I had resolved not to go back. What else could I do? I drove four hours and met my mom at John Muir Hospital. As I walked into her room, I was stunned to find her lying on the bed, IV in her hand, tubes in her nose, and machines monitoring her. She looked frailer and weaker than I had ever seen her in my life. It was like staring at some person I was certain I knew, but at the same time it felt like she was a stranger. She was so fragile and nearly incoherent from all the drugs the doctors pumped into her that she was barely able to talk.

I was shocked and couldn't help but agonize as to whether she was going to survive. I had heard so many horror stories about people being diagnosed with cancer only to find out later it had spread throughout their lymph nodes and was terminal. I was terrified that somehow she wasn't going to get better, that she'd be terribly sick or worse, die. I had never seen my mom in this state before. When she was diagnosed with MS, I didn't see her during her worst time. I couldn't even recall going to visit her in the hospital. Seeing her now was completely overwhelming.

Amidst all the distress, though, I couldn't believe no one else in my family was at the hospital. If I could drive all the way up from San Luis Obispo, why couldn't they drive fifteen minutes or even a half hour to see her? I became angry. Where was my dad? Where were my sisters? Their absence fueled my mother's dependency on me. What was I supposed to do now? Leave my life behind? Be her sole supporter? Why was my dad unable to be by her side? Why was he so selfish? Why did he dislike her so much that he couldn't, one time, make the sacrifice to be with her? Not even something like breast cancer could bring out the slightest bit of compassion in him. He's never going to change, I thought, he'll be selfish and uncaring forever.

So many thoughts raced through my mind as I watched my mom lay in silence. Would she get better once she had her mastectomy? Last month she seemed fine. How did she get cancer in the first place? Was I supposed to quit school to take care of her? I didn't have answers to anything. For now, I had to pretend to be strong and be by her side.

The mastectomy was a success. She didn't have any complications in surgery. Thankfully, her doctors were good surgeons. They believed her cancer had not spread to her lymph nodes, so she did not have to follow up with chemotherapy. Once the surgery was over, she needed a lot of rest. Still terribly weak from the operation and the medication, she could only lie in bed. For the most part, she either cried or slept. She was the thinnest I had ever seen her. She looked like an extremely frail old lady who if handled roughly, could easily break a bone. My mom was gaunt, as if the life had been sucked right out of her. It was so painful to see her in this state, so very sick. With no one to talk to, I deliberated whether I would be able to return to college. I wanted to continue pursuing an education despite my bulimia. I would do anything not to have to live at home. It made me sick to think of the possibility. I hoped my dad would step up, be a man, and take care of things, because she couldn't manage to do even the smallest things like grocery shopping or laundry.

I didn't have the answers, and I couldn't ask my dad or sisters for fear they'd attack me and make me feel selfish. My sisters—for reasons known only to them—thought my mom favored me over them. By default, they thought I should be the one to do whatever was needed at any given moment. My life was never as important as theirs.

I cringed at the thought of giving up everything to take care of her. I knew that would be my demise and the final victory for my bulimic self. After a few days at home with my mom, I came to realize that, despite how sick she was, I couldn't stay for good. If I did, the chances of both of us falling apart were greater. I was terribly hurt by all the years she never took care of me, especially when I asked for help with my disease, and how I always seemed to be either invisible or playing the mother in a bizarre role reversal. I felt as if I had been robbed of my childhood. Consequently, I wasn't emotionally stable enough myself to give her what she needed. After spending a few days in my old, miserable bedroom, I thought I'd die if I stayed. I told her I had to leave and could only hope that my dad and sisters would help out once I was gone.

Ironically years later my Mom would actually say to me (and later even to my current husband) that she believes she got cancer as a result of being so depressed at me leaving to go to college!

Chapter 13

The Fog Around the Sun

After two years at Poly, I decided I needed a change. I liked the college, but ever since the incident back in the dorms and my continual personal decline, I felt as if a fresh start might be just the thing for me. I traveled farther from my childhood home and transferred to San Diego State University.

Despite having very little information regarding San Diego and SDSU, I relied on my infrequent visits with friends there to be my guide and motivation to go. I planned on living in San Diego alone, without Matt. He was going to stay behind and try and get his GPA up at Cal Poly so he could transfer too. Once he accomplished this, he'd be able to be with me. I wasn't looking forward to having another period of time where we would have to engage in a long-distance relationship, but I knew I needed to go.

The final documents were completed and I was officially going to attend SDSU in the fall of 1988. Just a couple weeks later, Matt unexpectedly received notification from Cal Poly admissions and records that he was kicked out of the school. I hadn't realized how bad his grades were. He had lied to me, telling me he just needed to bring his GPA up a little. I was shocked by this news, even more so by the fact that he had lied to me about something so significant. But I also knew there was nothing I could do. Certainly I couldn't go to the dean of admissions and beg him to give Matt one more chance. Matt would join me in San Diego. His way of fixing the situation was to assure me that now it wouldn't be so hard a transition for me because he'd be with me.

San Diego was as lovely as I remembered it, with white, sandy beaches, blue skies, and endless boardwalks. There were all kinds of activities to enjoy from jogging, rollerblading, and people watching, to just taking in the beautiful scenery. It seemed almost magical because it was so beautiful to me. I sensed the people, especially the ones at the beach, were more relaxed and easygoing, far more so than the people in San Luis and especially more than those in San Francisco's East Bay. San Diego was like a melting pot of all different kinds of people, and I welcomed that. For once I was not afraid I wouldn't fit in and felt I'd made the right decision.

By looking through the Roommate Wanted section of the local newspaper, I secured a private room with a private bath, an absolute must for a hard-core bulimic like me, in a very nice housing unit just minutes away from campus. I couldn't afford to live on my own, so again, I had roommates.

I unpacked my bags and moved into Stonebridge Apartments where I'd share living quarters with Kylie and Sharon. At first things went as expected. Kylie, Sharon, and I chatted from time to time and occasionally watched TV together. But because I was so into my disease, I never opted to do much else with them. I never went to a movie or any event or out to eat with them. And I never joined them when they ordered take-out food for the apartment.

Kylie and Sharon never seemed bothered about my not going out with them but in terms of my food, they weren't as discrete. They recognized pretty quickly that I had very strange eating habits, so once the awkwardness of living with a new roommate was over, they had no qualms about making the odd remark. Rather than replying or trying to defend myself, I just blew them off or changed the subject. They had been friends long before I met them, and I wasn't looking to make friends with them. We were very different, and even if we weren't, it was virtually impossible for me to get too close to anyone other than Matt. One person was all I could handle. More than that would be too difficult for me to deal with while struggling with my disease. After a couple months passed, I tried to avoid Kylie and Sharon as much as possible. Better than having to face any negativity, I thought.

My relationship with bulimia progressed. I binged and purged several times a day, having discovered a brand new set of drive-by places to frequent. My intake of diet and water pills was almost countless. Whenever I felt overwhelmed or anxious, I'd pop a couple in my mouth. What changed was I no longer felt relief from my usual laxative, so I tried taking mineral oil, something I discovered while shopping in Longs Drugs for my usual OTC pills. I took a spoonful in the morning and evening, careful to conceal what I was doing. I found by doing this, I experienced faster results. I quickly became addicted. Still laser-focused on becoming thinner, I combined the three most effective methods of elimination for maximum effect: purging, exercising, and using laxatives. I was determined the calories would come out of me one way or another, either in vomit, sweat, or feces. It amazes me there are still people who consider bulimia a "glamorous" disorder. The reality is degrading and foul.

I felt like my entire world would come crashing down if I didn't work out, so I joined a twenty-four-hour Nautilus my first day in San Diego. I never allowed myself an excuse not to work out. Sick, injured, or otherwise, if I wasn't lying in a hospital bed then there was no good reason not to go to the gym. To rationalize this, I considered working out as my therapy.

Kylie, Sharon, and I were becoming more like complete strangers than roommates. By midyear we rarely spoke to one another, or they never spoke to me. There was so much tension between us it was like walking on eggshells all the time. I'd had enough. I couldn't live that way anymore. It was time for me to move on once again.

Bulimics are often lonely, isolated people. We are afraid of relationships as they threaten to expose our true nature, our compulsions, and our disease. Secrecy is more important than intimacy. So when I made friends with a girl at the gym, it was quite out of character for me. After casually talking for a while, we soon learned that we lived in the same complex and we were both unhappy with our roommate situation. Without knowing each other—we had hung out together just a few times—we decided to get a place together.

After committing to this new arrangement, I panicked. I wasn't sure if I'd be able to hide my bulimia from her. *What am I thinking? I don't know her. We've barely spent any time together. Suppose she turns out to be a crazy witch? Suppose I don't have the privacy I need for my bulimia because we are much friendlier than I have been with any of my roommates?* I was stuck now. I closed my eyes and hoped for the best.

Within a month, Jackie and I lugged our belongings across the road. Our new apartment was a far cry from the nice, plush complex we had just left. This apartment and the entire complex were dark and dreary. The carpet was an unattractive dark brown and regardless of the time of day, no light shone through the few windows. At first we laughed it off, but not too long after moving in, we decided it was just too depressing to stay more than the remaining school year. To make our stay more palatable, Jackie and I decided we'd party all the time to help forget about the dreariness of the place. Jackie was a bigger partier than I was so between her and Matt, who was always partying, I never lacked party companionship.

Jackie and I had no problems getting along. We had an immediate connection. And without any discussion, we knew when to give each other space. Living with her was easy, and whatever reservations I once harbored quickly evaporated. The level of friendship I could offer Jackie seemed to work for both us and did not intrude on my deeper relationship with my bulimic self.

I vowed to make the best of our living situation. Our apartment was the most depressing place I had ever lived in. It made my Alamo home look like a palace, and that wasn't saying much. We continued our parade of partying nonstop. We'd smoke pot constantly and drink occasionally. To reach an even higher level of bliss, we started taking harder drugs, namely speed and crystal methamphetamine. I had tried coke before, but these tonics were far more powerful and the high lasted far longer. I quickly fell in love with both of them. Now I was wired all the time and felt like I had an endless supply of energy, great for working out, but best of all, I had no appetite. This was absolutely fantastic for me, a dream come true. I didn't have to worry about binging and purging everything I ate because I rarely ate if I had drugs. It was as if I had found a cure for my bulimia. Instead of gorging on everything in sight, I could restrict my food intake with ease and not have to suffer the gnawing hunger that had previously accompanied those efforts. The drugs made it easy and effortless for me to eat between eight hundred and eleven hundred calories a day.

With this powerful new ally by my side, I could finally lose weight without relying only on binging and purging or diet pills. No longer did I have to waste hours and hours a day shoving my fingers down my throat, waiting for the food to come back up. Sure enough, after a period of continually doing these drugs, I lost weight. I reached one hundred nine pounds. I was happy and didn't care whether my daily habit was potentially harming. I cared only about getting thin. Not only did I lose weight, but my hours of exercising were effortless, my room was always immaculate, and I focused harder on my studies. By the end of the semester, while doing speed and crystal meth, I completed fifteen units and received a 3.80 GPA. I made SDSU's Dean's List for academic achievement. I felt good about myself, something I hadn't felt in a very long time.

Intellectually, I wasn't ignorant to the fact there was a huge downside to taking drugs. Speed and crystal weren't going to do me any favors in the long run. Eventually, after my honeymoon period with them, I began to slide back into my bulimia. I knew all my partying served only as a cover up for my true addiction. With my highs came lows. When the effects of the drugs wore off, the ecstasy and energy would disappear, and I'd feel depressed and withdrawn. For months and months I rode this rollercoaster. I needed a break. By the end of that semester, we all committed to cutting back on our intake.

I was happy with my grades and ready to move on. Jackie and I decided we had had enough living near campus. We needed to move to the beach. We found an apartment on Ocean Boulevard in the heart of Mission Beach. It was a great location, walking distance to everything except school, but I didn't care about that. We were looking forward to living at the beach and also to living with our soon-to-be new roommate, Monica. Monica often came over to the ugly, dreary apartment, and I knew she would become a good friend, just like Jackie. Our new home would be 1001 Island Boulevard and Ocean Front Walk.

It was summertime when we moved into our airy, second floor apartment, with its windows facing the ocean. We all loved living there. Jackie, Monica, and I sat on our patio or the ocean wall and observed all the strange and wonderful people pass by. Every night as the sun would disappear, we'd watch happily as if each sunset was the first we'd ever seen. I felt incredibly calm and free, something to do with the ocean. And I loved the beach far more than I ever imagined. I felt comfortable, like I finally fit in, especially with all the different kinds of characters that milled about me.

I continued to work at the surf shop where I had started in the latter part of the school year, only now I took on a full-time shift. This was the best job I'd had so far, head and shoulders above all the jobs I'd had before. I sold mostly men's and some women's surf and skate clothing and worked with a great group of laid-back guys and girls. Even my boss was cool. Because I loved it so much, I never minded having to work. I excelled at selling and was making fairly good money. While most people I worked with made about seven dollars an hour, I was making between twelve and fifteen. I felt like I was taking home big bucks. I loved seeing the monetary reward for a job well done. It gave me a level of confidence I had never had before. As soon as I'd get my paycheck, I'd spend it. I was never good at keeping money but at that time, I was doing a good job making it. My checks covered everything from my bills to clothes and, most importantly, my food. Although I felt much happier and more peaceful it only helped finance my bulimia, but didn't contribute to overcoming it. And if Matt didn't know before, he did now.

In a heated moment while we visited home one weekend, my sister Susan shouted at him "Matt, Jocelyn is bulimic. You know what that means. She eats tons of food and then goes and throws it up. Sick, huh?" She did this to try to ruin the best thing, the only thing, I had, in the hope he'd break up with me once my secret was revealed. This wouldn't be the last time she tried ruining one of my relationships.

Matt didn't break up with me, but he said nothing about it to me afterwards either. Since he didn't seem to care, I thought it would be the best time to confess to my roommates that I had some "food issues" and I was kind of bulimic at times, rather than let them draw their own conclusions, whatever they might be. In reality, though, my bizarre eating rituals were too obvious to miss after any length of time living in close quarters with me. They were dealing with their own crises and demons, and they didn't care either, which left me feeling relieved. Perfect, I thought, now I can go on and eat and do my thing without worrying about being discovered. Although I hid my bulimic rituals from them, I found it easier to deal with the obvious other behaviors such as eating only certain foods, refusing to eat out, taking pills, and exercising compulsively, or sharing in dinner preparation, especially if I knew I couldn't keep down whatever it was they were making. I was becoming used to living with bulimia and figured this was how the rest of my life would be. It had become normal to me.

When I wasn't working a shift at the surf shop, I spent my time tanning on the beach or sitting in front of our apartment complex watching the crowds of people. By now my two roommates, Matt, and I had resumed our partying and were constantly finding new ways to have fun. There was an endless supply of drugs and alcohol flowing through our place. Because our ocean-front apartment was in a very accessible location, it became a mini Grand Central Station. Everyone we collectively knew and even people we didn't know would come by daily to hang out with us. Surprisingly, I found this exciting and loved having people around all the time. I'd spent so much of my life isolated that I welcomed the intrusions and chaos and everyone's good mood. It wasn't like anything I had experienced before.

Although on one level I was having the time of my life, I couldn't overcome my continual obsessions with my body image and food. I never stopped feeling complete terror over gaining weight, so I tried restricting my food intake as much as possible when I wasn't binging and purging. Ever since I'd gone on my first diet at Diet Center, I would go through phases of eating only certain types of food that I deemed safe. That summer and the following school year was one of those times I did just that, eating the same foods each day and rarely, if ever, straying from them. I allowed myself to have a plain water bagel and some malted milk balls for my morning meal, a nonfat frozen yogurt for lunch—no toppings and definitely never a regular or low-fat flavor—and either a Weight Watchers or Lean Cuisine frozen dinner. When I'd get sick of eating those, I'd have a salad with plain vinegar dressing in the evenings. About one thousand calories, I calculated. I was running on pure adrenaline, trying to keep up with work, exercising, and my social life. I slept only about five hours a night, but I didn't find this difficult, even after classes began. The only change in my routine was I decreased my working hours to between twenty-five and thirty to accommodate my full load at SDSU. I was able to manage my schedule and the long hours because my surf shop hours never varied—Monday, Wednesday, and Friday evenings and all day Saturday and Sunday.

During the year, my weight fluctuated constantly. I couldn't always be diligent about restricting, and I just wasn't completely anorexic, so my weight never stayed the same. If I was faithful at restricting, I'd lose weight. If I binged and purged, I'd gain. In the end, I lost and gained back over thirty pounds. I went from size one to size seven. As I continued to ride my roller coaster of restriction and intense bulimia, my emotions, too, were on the same roller coaster. I grew more self-conscious, self-doubting, insecure, and guarded. The visitors started becoming too much for me now. And where I had once found peace and solace by the ocean, I became lost in my bulimic fog.

No matter where I lived or worked—we all eventually moved on and went our separate ways—my bulimia followed. I continued with the same behavior as always. The more years I struggled with the disease, the easier it became to hide it and the more creative I became at finding ways to binge and purge. I continued to abuse myself daily through bulimia and its related behaviors and my dependency on laxatives grew. I binged and purged not just in the confinement of my home or a public restroom, but I purged at work as well, something very risky. I had reached a point where if I decided I was going to binge, then nothing and nobody could stop me.

Matt and I leased our own apartment my last year at SDSU. We'd been dating for nearly six years when we moved into a complex in Pacific Beach, just a few short minutes from my old place in Mission Beach. Many of our friends lived here, so again there were constantly people hanging out at our place. Most nights we'd all get together in our front courtyard and have small parties and barbeques, unless we were having a bonfire on the beach. Even more so than before, there always seemed to be something going on. I had far more acquaintances than I ever had and felt more like I was accepted for who I was, and not the fat school girl who always haunted me. But I still couldn't fully enjoy the company of others. I continued to turn inward and recoil rather than reach outward and embrace people. I just couldn't fully trust anyone other than my bulimic self. Even Matt, despite my loving him, held a distant second to my disease. Often, while hanging out with the neighbors, I'd run in the apartment, ingest whatever foods I could, go back outside, and pretend I'd done a quick chore. Then I'd make up some excuse why I had to go indoors again and throw up the food I'd just eaten.

As I was putting my three fingers down my throat, my neighbors would be socializing right outside the front door. Why couldn't I just hang out like the rest of them? Why did I always run inside and secretly devour what I could find? Why couldn't I relax and just be one of the gang like I so desperately wanted to be? No matter what the circumstances, good or bad, I somehow turned to bulimia as a means of coping with my inability to understand my feelings, my situation, and the nightmares of the past that continued to haunt me. It seemed as if I could just not offer myself the gift of happiness. Nothing but bulimia entered or survived in my inner world. To mask any noise I might make, I ran the water in the sink full blast. Often Matt knew why I was heading indoors while he stayed outside enjoying himself, but he just accepted it. Without ever communicating, we acknowledged my bulimia by my saying, "I had a bad day." Usually he'd respond with, "It will be okay." This was more feedback than I'd received to date and I settled for that.

When I graduated from college, I felt I had achieved a major milestone in my life. I was now a college graduate. In high school, I didn't think I would ever accomplish something like this. I looked forward to receiving my diploma. It never occurred to me that my parents or Matt would not want to attend the ceremony. I read all the material regarding the service and called home. "Mom, graduation is almost here," I said to her when she answered the phone. Her reply cut through me like a knife.

"Great. I'm sure you don't care if Dad and I don't come down for the ceremony. We didn't go to Susan's and she didn't seem to mind."

What could I say? "No, actually I am very disappointed. I can't believe this means so little to you. After all, back when I was so frightened to go away and confessed that I was bulimic, you seemed to think it was a 'very big deal' getting a college degree." Instead, I simply replied that I didn't mind. Again I tried to appease her even though it meant neglecting my hurt and my own feelings. She didn't seem to care enough to support me or celebrate this very important event in my life. Once more, I felt like whatever I did it wasn't worthy of her or my dad's time. It was just an inconvenience she'd rather not endure. As for Matt, he never even offered to come. Disappointed by my mom's lack of support, I said nothing to Matt. I pretended it didn't matter. With no one to attend, I didn't have the heart to go alone. Months later I received my diploma in the mail.

After graduation, I began to wonder what I was going to do with my life. No sooner did I begin thinking and stressing about it when Susan, who was a successful Silicon Valley software sales rep, and my dad started calling me constantly. "Jocelyn, what are you going to do now? You need to get a real job and quit working in those beach shops. You'll never make any money. They're dumb jobs and you need to grow up." I felt I wasn't ready for this, I needed more time. I was completely bulimic.

My dad always followed suit. "Jocelyn, I've just spoken to Susan, we agree you need to get a real job now. I've worked non-stop since I was in my early twenties. I think you should get into sales like Susan." It was true. My father had never taken a holiday in all the years I was growing up, work being his drug of choice. Too shy and self-conscious to argue with them or look to Matt for comfort as he wouldn't have had an opinion, I felt like I had no other choice but to agree to whatever they had decided was best for me. It seemed rather bizarre that suddenly the two of them were taking an interest in my life, not in a supportive way, but rather, in a condescending and disrespectful way. They pretty much considered my life to be a joke, and they were intervening to set me right.

I embarked on an intensive job search. One interview after another, one screw up after screw up, I never managed to get a real job until the day I answered an ad in the paper that said: "Wanted: Entry level sales position. To sell warehouse equipment such as nuts, bolts, screws in the San Diego area." I wanted to please my dad and sister, rather than Matt, who was increasingly retreating into his own world of drugs and isolation, so I reluctantly called the number. I'd had many interviews by now and felt pretty confident at talking my way through one or at least not screwing it up too much. I got the job, even though I didn't want it. In fact, I wanted to stay at my bikini shop job where, for the past year and a half, I was assistant manager right across the street from where I lived. But I knew that wasn't good enough for my family, and I wanted to please them. I wanted them to think more highly of me and accept me.

My new boss gave me a roll of dimes each day to make cold calls from the local pay phone. Just as I figured, I hated it. It was lonely, and I hated trying to make appointments from a phone booth with people listening to my calls while waiting. I didn't know the first thing about garage-type equipment. I probably used a hammer a handful of times in my life, let alone a butt-connector or high-powered torch. If I actually secured a face-to-face appointment, I felt more like the village idiot than a sales rep. More often than not, the guys in the garage shops would end up doing my demo for me. All in all, it was a disaster. I stomached the grueling job for about two months, living out of my car. Eventually I couldn't take it any longer and I quit. I was too miserable to worry about pleasing my family. Naturally, they were angry with me and had no problems sharing their feelings. "Why, Jocelyn? It was a good job, not a dumb job like selling bikinis. You have graduated from college now. You need to live in the real world." Real world? My real world was bulimia. I was barely making it through a day without intense pain in my stomach, blood and bile coming up, and uncontrollable diarrhea. I couldn't concentrate or get excited about selling junk to warehousemen. Their comments only added to my feelings of humiliation.

Once I quit, Matt proposed to me. After almost seven years together, he finally asked me to marry him. My spirits lifted—I was very happy. I couldn't imagine my life without him. I was entirely codependent on him, regardless of the shallowness of our relationship. It mattered little to me that Matt never got intimately involved in my life or that he ignored my bulimia. I only cared about the need to feel loved and wanted. For that, I would sacrifice everything else.

I finally secured a job selling women's clothing at a well-known retail store in La Jolla. Relieved to go back to what I knew best, selling clothes, I looked forward to this job. As the new girl, it was only fair I work the worst shifts, mostly nights and every weekend with no day off. But I thought it was better than not having a job, and I needed money for my living expenses and binges.

By the end of the first day I knew I had a challenge on my hands. The girls who had been working there before me were less than welcoming. They were more like wicked bitches from hell and did everything possible to make my life miserable. They scheduled me for twice the amount of labor work—stocking and cleaning, which eats into commissioned selling time—and constantly belittled my every move. They rarely spoke to me unless it was to criticize. I hated working there. What I'd thought would be a good job turned into a total nightmare. I couldn't quit, and I felt like a complete imbecile, a college graduate who couldn't even sell the easiest of things, women's clothing in a retail store. I never said anything in my defense. I worked twice as hard as anyone there, which meant less time selling, fewer commissions, and increased possibility of being fired for not reaching my quota. I reached out, once again, to my friend, bulimia, and numbed the days with binge and purge sessions in the store's bathrooms.

Besides the money, another benefit of my new job was having the mornings free. While Matt was off working, I could go for a long run—sometimes up to nine miles—and binge and purge as much as I desired with total privacy. Then off to work I would go, feeling exhausted. Working as hard as I could while trying to achieve sales, I'd grow more fatigued. Sometimes I wouldn't eat at all during my nine-hour shift, relying on numerous cups of coffee to get through. By eleven p.m. when I finished, I'd be famished, a toxic state for a bulimic. I'd stop off at several different fast-food eateries on the way home. If that wasn't enough, I'd grab the food stocked in our kitchen. Then I'd head off to the bathroom where I'd watch it all go down the toilet. I never knew if Matt noticed or heard me throwing up since he never said anything. I assumed either he chose not to or he couldn't be bothered. Sometimes I wanted him to reach out and hear my cries for help. But he never did. I knew it was impossible for me to overcome this addiction alone or through sheer willpower. Knowing it was self-destructive was no match for the grip it had over me.

After a couple months I was still working at the same store. As unhappy and worthless as I felt, I tried to pretend it didn't matter to me. I had Matt and that's all I believed I needed. But with our wedding approaching, I began to go through what all brides-to-be do, I worried about my weight and how I would look. To most people, this does not take on the significance it did for me, but I was too fat. I had gained weight since graduation and was now utterly ashamed at how I looked. I couldn't walk down the aisle like that. So I began a crazy ride of trying to lose weight at all costs. I increased my use of diet pills, water pills, and laxatives to ten, twelve, sometimes fifteen of each. I was now experiencing constant abdominal pain and losing control of my bowels every so often. I told myself over and over again it didn't matter as I tried to dismiss the intense pain. I needed to lose weight before my wedding day. Whatever it took, I was willing to try. Matt and I still partied with hard drugs occasionally, so I relied on the same old false promises coke and crystal meth offered. Doing them as much as possible, I prayed for a weight loss miracle, I prayed they'd transform me, and I'd wake up thin and pretty, then maybe even the girls at the store would have more respect for me. I believed if I were thin and pretty like them, they wouldn't be so mean to me.

Constantly fighting my inner pains and demons, I achieved a small weight loss—six to seven pounds —but at the price of complete exhaustion and depression. I began thinking I'd never be able to stay thin and that meant I'd never be truly happy. The girls at work, I convinced myself, noticed my dieting and went so far as to comment on how I looked better. During work, I'd eat only a small cup of rice but when not at work, I'd binge and purge with all manner of food, excessively use drugs, and exercise like a maniac, all in the unshakable belief that thinness was my ticket to happiness.

Reflecting back on the nearly seven years Matt and I dated, I realized we never went out to a formal dinner. He never invited me and I never asked. Although I was too afraid of the hidden calories in any foods other than those I prepared or bought after studying their labels, sometimes I had fleeting moments where I wished he would have at least asked me out to a nice restaurant. I hoped for some kind of reassurance that I was fine just the way I was, but I never received this reassurance, even though he knew I replaced bulimia with dieting.

Our wedding day finally arrived, May 15, 1993. Because both our parents were in Northern California, we decided it would be easier to have our wedding there. We were married at eleven at St. Isidore's Church, the same church attached to the school I had attended growing up. Thankfully, I didn't come across dear Sister Mary!

We were on a limited budget of two thousand dollars that covered everything from my dress to the cost of the priest, so we held the reception at my parent's house. I wanted to embrace the day like a normal bride, but I couldn't. I was extremely fatigued from the intense dieting and pill abuse leading up to this moment. My inner bulimic self screamed out to me, "Jocelyn, you are too fat. Look at you in that dress. You're busting out of it. You will look back on this day for the rest of your life with regret for not losing enough weight." I was so into my disease that not even my wedding day could tear me from the spell it had cast over me. Trying as best I could to hide my feelings from Matt and every one else, I acted as the happy, smiling bride people expected. I wanted to eat, in fact, I was starving. But I didn't know what to do. Could I control myself? Could I let go just for this one very special day? The catered food looked so good and I was so hungry that by three, I couldn't resist. Piece by piece, I placed the tasty morsels on my plate and ate it all, one spoonful after another. I was overcome with guilt. *Jocelyn, you blew it. All that hard work down the drain. Now you will go off on your honeymoon and be just as fat as you were before.*

My feeling of guilt increased as the celebration wound down and our wedding night beckoned. At what was supposed to be a special moment, my bulimia gatecrashed the party. Instead of having a romantic night with my new husband, I ran into the bathroom and threw up. Matt was disappointed. There was no denying the look on his face. I couldn't think clearly after the day's stress and had to find some kind of relief. The only way I knew how was to eat and throw up. I ruined a night that could never be recaptured.

Our honeymoon was no exception. I couldn't escape from my bulimia. Despite playing at the beach, snorkeling, and sightseeing in Ixtapa, Mexico, I binged and purged every morning and evening. After eating breakfast together, I'd tell Matt I was stepping out to buy a magazine or get a newspaper. Instead, I bought all kinds of Mexican pastries at the store located in the main lobby of our hotel room. I'd run into one of the public bathrooms where I'd shove handful after handful of fluffy and very dry pastries and cookies down my throat. Then I'd return to our room and while Matt sat on the patio taking in the beautiful ocean scenery, I'd eat the rest of whatever I bought, in the bathroom, and immediately throw it all up. I made up my usual excuse, hoping he wasn't aware of what I was doing. I told him I had an upset stomach, and I needed some privacy. He didn't question me. It was the same routine at night. Even if I couldn't make it to the local convenience store, I had to find a bathroom and throw up anything I ate. I couldn't focus on my new life. My disease was the most important thing to me, whether I wanted it to be or not.

Chapter 14

The Bitterest End

Before Matt and I got married, I urged him to move back to Northern California. I had become convinced that we both needed to be nearer our families now that we were married, but most of all I thought it would help Matt get his life straightened out. He was still addicted to drugs and continued to run away from his demons by avoiding reality. Between his drug habit and my food addictions, we were continually broke. I thought he could get a better job in the Bay Area even though he had not graduated college. In fact, he had lied to me for three semesters, telling me he was attending classes when he was at friends' places getting high. He even set off in the morning with books under his arm. Such was the nature of our crazy relationship.

As I look back, I understand I was naïve or in denial. He never paid the bills and avoided any type of responsibility. His only concern was having enough money for dope and time for surfing. I always managed to convince myself none of this mattered, that I needed only love. My parents had no love and they were completely miserable even with a house and my dad's good job. I certainly didn't want to end up like them, so I tried to overlook my stoned husband's slacker ways.

Reluctantly, Matt agreed to relocate and soon we moved to back up to Northern California where we found an impressive apartment in Foster City. It had two bedrooms—one for my workout equipment—a big family room, kitchen, and bathroom. There was an eleven-mile bike path along the lagoon, just a five-minute walk from our apartment, where we could run, ride bikes, or roller blade. We could surf and even water ski with Susan, who lived only a few miles away.

As I mentioned before, bulimics have this great capacity for temporary blind optimism and for setting ourselves up for massive falls. One of the great paradoxes of this disease is that emotions are always extreme. Bulimics are either totally up or completely down, and these conditions are interchangeable at a moment's notice. So it wasn't surprising that I told myself this would be a new beginning. I would get my bulimia under control and we would have a happy married life.

Still, a day didn't go by without my binging and purging. I was able to keep my retail job by transferring to a store near our new place, but I had to start over again, working the late shift, etc. Matt found a job with a moving company. I had so much alone time that I fell deeper into the dangerous claws of my bulimia. I would consume up to two loaves of bread in the morning along with several bowls of cereal. Sometimes I would even eat bowls of vegetables on top of bread, believing that this was better for me than cereal. My food combinations were getting stranger and stranger. I didn't care. I was going to throw it all up anyway.

I was now consuming such large quantities of food, I would use a plastic bag to gather my purge, afraid I'd clog the toilet and have to call the landlord. No way was I willing to try and explain that. I'd take the putrid bag out to the dumpster just behind our building and discard it there. I'd eat and eat and throw up so many times before my shift started that my face would swell up and I'd look like a chipmunk. I was so fatigued it was almost a miracle I made it to work in the first place. Nighttime was no exception. More often than not, Matt would come home well after me, so I had all the time in the world to engage in and intensify my bulimic endeavors.

As time passed, Matt and I saw less of each other. I was so dependent on him—he was the only friend I had—that I found this separation extremely difficult. Why was he coming home so late? Where once he had been returning around eleven or midnight, the norm was now becoming two or three in the morning, sleep a couple hours, and then leave at five a.m. He would tell me he was working on a big job and these were the hours he had to pull. I wanted to believe him, so I'd accept his explanations, looking the other way. I needed him and the thought of being alone was beyond terrifying. I would put up with anything to appease him, even if that meant hardly seeing him. I didn't want to start a fight. I feared that might lead to his leaving for good. Apart from an occasional plea for him to spend time with me, I said nothing.

One day, however, when I sat down to pay our bills, I could no longer avoid confronting Matt. To my horror, our entire savings—three thousand two hundred dollars we had received as wedding gifts—was gone. The bank balance indicated thirty-two dollars in our account. I confronted Matt as he walked in the door after work. He casually admitted he had spent it all on cocaine. He apologized, but didn't seem unduly concerned or contrite. I couldn't believe it. In one month he had spent all the money we had. "Do you know how much coke you had to have snorted?" I asked. "Do you realize that it's like an eight ball a day?

Don't you care about us? How are we going to live? How are we going to pay the bills?" After an interlude in which I cried and he sat and stared in silence, he asked for forgiveness and I, as usual, succumbed and forgave him.

More immediately upsetting was the fact we were going to have to find another place to live. We couldn't afford Foster City any longer. In fact, we couldn't afford anywhere now. As usual I convinced myself that due to my bulimia and my general unworthiness as a person, I couldn't afford to lose him and would do whatever I needed to fix things.

So after a year in Foster City, Matt and I packed our bags and headed to Alamo. We had nowhere else to go and no money saved. The only option was to move into my parent's house for a short while. Once again, I was back in my ugly brown bedroom and the house I loathed so much. I was grateful I could tell my parents the truth, that Matt had snorted all our money, but their reaction was a few consoling words and then they went on as if nothing had happened. It seemed to me at this stage they'd rather turn a blind eye than get involved—too much trouble to put themselves out for anyone other than themselves. My heart cared little that Matt had snorted all our money away. What bothered me most was that the knowledge he didn't care about me or our marriage, but I set aside the truth and tried to make the best of our new situation. I secured a job with the same retail chain in another store near the house.

From the first day Matt and I stayed at my parent's house, I knew it was going to be a bumpy ride. Matt went to work for another moving company. He'd lost the prior one, I suspect, sometime before the coke binge that financially ruined us. Like his previous job, he was going to work long hours. To add to that, the company was located in South San Francisco, which meant a long commute from the East Bay. Were we ever going to see each other? Did Matt even care? I was too afraid to ask him.

As time wore on, I spent even more time alone than I did back in Foster City. Matt regularly called and said he wouldn't be home because he had a late finish and an early start and it was easier to crash at a friend's in the city. Sometimes he'd be gone for only one night, other times two. I cried and cried and didn't know what to do. Should I believe that he was just too tired from working to drive all the way back to Alamo? Do I insist that he come home? Do I say nothing and tell him I love him? I elected to do just that, because I wanted to believe he was working hard for us, that he, too, wanted to move out of my parent's house and start to live like a real married couple. Still, I resented the fact I was stuck in my parent's house thanks to his drug habit and selfishness, yet he rarely stayed there. I was terribly lonely now and had no one to confide in. I knew Matt and I were living a false married life. While I was trying to pull him into the marriage, Matt was trying to pull out. It was clear I was miserable, but I didn't know how much Matt was. For now, I would settle for my relationship with my bulimic self. I would binge and purge, exercise, and use and abuse laxatives to numb myself and shut out the feelings of hurt and abandonment.

Things got progressively worse. My dad was back in Atlanta working, coming home roughly once a month. My mom had decided she no longer liked Alamo and packed her bags to go live in Mexico for part of the year. She'd been doing this for a couple years by the time Matt and I moved in. Matt would rarely show up or spend time with me. On one occasion he told me he was going snowboarding with some friends in Tahoe and he'd be home the next day. But several days passed and no calls, no messages on the answering machine. Day four he showed up and said, "I figured you'd be angry with me so I didn't bother calling. I didn't want you to ruin my fun." Still I hung in, hoping for a sudden change, hoping that he loved me, and hoping I could get my bulimia under control.

On Friday, July 29, 1995, around six, I was working the late shift at the store when the phone rang. "Hi, it's me," said Matt. "How's work going? How are your sales today? Listen, I just called to say hi, but I gotta to go. It's too hot to talk now. Bye." I tried to keep him on the line, but he was gone. What did he mean "it was too hot to talk?" What did the heat have to do with talking on the phone? Why didn't he tell me he loved me? He had never forgotten to tell me he loved me in all the conversations we'd had through all our years together. I tried to dismiss the discomfort I felt from our brief conversation until my shift ended.

I drove home to easy listening music, assuring myself I'd soon see Matt and my unease would disappear. The front door was locked. Strange, I thought. Oh, well, Matt must be downstairs watching TV. He'd also forgotten to leave the front porch light on for me.

I never noticed his truck was missing. I opened the big brown door and switched on the hall light. That's when I saw it, a note that changed my life: *Dear Jocelyn, We've been together a very long time, almost nine years and I think you are a good person. But I don't love you any more. Find someone else. Someone who can appreciate you and love you better than I could. Don't wait for me. I am not coming back. I need to move and not be with you. Forget about me because I don't love you anymore.*

His wedding ring, the house keys, the credit cards, and checkbook all lay beside the note. Nearly nine years together, then this. I fell to my knees, barely able to breathe. I read and reread the note. As tears raced down my cheeks, my breathing became intense and choppy. It then sunk in that Matt had left me. He was gone. He said he didn't love me. My worst fear had come true. In my heart I knew he was never coming back. That's why he'd acted so strangely on the phone. That's why he said he "couldn't talk any longer because it was too hot." He was packing his bags to head out the door, out of my life forever. I didn't care. I wanted him back. I would do anything for him, just like I always had. Hysterical and with no one at home, I phoned the police, hoping they'd find him and bring him home. They said they could do nothing. I phoned his mom, hopeful she knew something, but she didn't. Then I called Susan.

Part of me died right then and there. I felt like I was alive on the outside but dead on the inside. I cared little that our married life was less than perfect. Matt had made me feel that he loved me, and even if it was just a little, that was enough for me, or at least more than I had felt my entire life. He was my best friend, my only friend, my first boyfriend, my first everything. Life as I knew it was now turned completely upside down. I was alone, confused, inconsolable, and abandoned. What was I going to do?

That night, Susan helped me pack some bags and took me to her house in Foster City. I couldn't spend another minute in that old dismal house on Austin Lane. It harbored my most horrific memories of bulimia, my family, and now the loss of the only man I had ever loved.

Distraught and in complete despair, I had no idea what lay ahead for me. Day after day I lay in bed crying for Matt. I pleaded with God, promised him the moon, if only he'd bring Matt back to me. Why hadn't Matt ever talked to me? Why hadn't he shared how unhappy he was? Why didn't he want to try and work things out with me, change things for us? So many thoughts raced through my head that my thinking became confused and incoherent. I had done everything in my power to make things right, fix all the messes he alone had gotten us into such as when he neglected to tell me he stopped making car insurance payments for two years and I negotiated with Nissan for a payment plan. He walked out on jobs, never bothering to tell me the truth or even tell me at all sometimes. He received an upfront payment from a Catholic church in Oakland for a job he never did, in essence stealing from them. I had overlooked, forgiven, dismissed, and taken care of so much because I was desperate to feel love no matter how little or how conditional. Although we were obviously codependent, I still believed I loved him unconditionally. I forgave him time and again because whenever he spoke to me, it was always to say nice things, and he never uttered a cross word. He'd never been unkind to me like my family or my classmates or even the women at the stores where I worked. I tried to be the perfect, all-loving, all-forgiving girlfriend and wife. I was too distraught to recognize the deeper truth, that I forgave him his transgressions because I was unable to give up my own, my self-destructive eating behavior.

This was the second time in my life I felt I needed to turn to my mom for help. She'd failed me on the first real occasion, when I told her I was bulimic, but now I was ready to give her a second chance to help me. I called her in Mexico and asked her to come home. "Jocelyn, I just got down here two weeks ago," she said. "It's so much work to pack all my things and travel back to Alamo. Can't you deal with this without me? Surely you can understand my situation?"

What, I said to myself, am I hearing this right? I was screaming and crying on the inside. Couldn't she see what this meant to me? My husband left me. He had gone into our room, sorted through everything we had acquired over the nearly nine years we'd spent together, picked and selected what he wanted, shipped the items he couldn't carry, and charged up the credit cards, leaving them for me to pay off. Not even Matt's abandoning me could prompt my mom to display some level of selflessness. I was completely crushed. I couldn't believe she cared only about herself and couldn't be bothered with me, especially considering how utterly devastating and life-altering this whole situation was.

As usual, I buried my feelings and simply said, "Sure, Mom, I understand. Don't worry, I'll be fine." After that brief exchange, I hung up the phone, crawled into bed, and started crying again. The level of importance my mom placed on my happiness and well-being had not changed any since I was the little fat girl crying in my room, vainly hoping she would come and explain all the craziness to me.

I went on a leave of absence from work for several weeks, spending my days in bed, crying and trying to figure out how to pick up the pieces of my life. I felt utter loneliness and isolation. The most pressing issue was finances. I knew Matt and I had no money saved despite not paying rent for the year we had lived in my parent's house, but as I started to sift through credit cards and bank statements, things went from bad to much, much worse. Bills started arriving, followed by phone calls from collection agencies. He had left us twenty-two thousand dollars in debt. The situation seemed hopeless given that I made only twenty-four thousand a year working at the retail store. The credit card companies wanted their money. Even the Diamond Center wanted payment for my wedding ring. There were monies owed to various people, the Catholic Church, and other vendors for work paid for but not done. To cap it all, there was a bill from the Fed Ex store for Matt's shipment of the things he couldn't carry out of my parent's house when he left. With a seemingly endless array of bills arriving, I was forced to cash in nearly five years of my 401(k) savings and profit sharing to help clear some of the debt. I sold all our furniture and belongings and even our wedding rings. My dad contributed five thousand dollars as his way of offering some kind of support. Even with all that, it wasn't enough. I had to pay for my normal costs of living, rent, and household bills at Susan's house. I was a mess. My money situation was a mess. At twenty-five, I felt like a worn-out, old woman. Drained and depressed, my emotions ran rampant. The only thing I felt I had left that was mine was my bulimia. Soon, we would begin a new dance that would take me to death's door.

I needed a job that paid more than what I could make selling women's clothing and after looking for a while, I was offered a position in telesales at a Fortune 500 company, the number one video and PC gaming company in the market. As I didn't have a clue what I was doing, I basically faked my way through the interview and then the first couple months on the job. I was glad to have found a professional position but because I had no experience in a corporate environment, my starting salary was only twenty-seven thousand, not much more than what I made at the retail store. Still optimistic, I stretched my money as far as possible. But my efforts weren't going to get me ahead and out of debt. I needed to earn more. My only option was to go to another outlet of the retail store directly up the road from my gaming job and Susan's house and get evening and weekend work. So my new life began—a full day at the computer company and then to the store for the evening shift. When Friday came, while others eagerly chatted about what fun activities they had planned, I could only look forward to a whole weekend of selling women's apparel.

In the few months after Matt left, I continued to be in a funk. Susan tried to lift my spirits by treating me to a holiday at Club Med in Cancun, Mexico. I didn't feel very upbeat, but I tried to make the best of it. I was grateful she went out of her way to try and help me have some fun, even though emotionally and mentally I was still having a hard time. To my very great surprise, I met a guy on our last night there.

Lance was nothing like Matt. He worked as a manager for a large Fortune 100 company, was nearly finished obtaining his MBA from Santa Clara University, and was well-spoken and refined. I couldn't figure out why he would be interested in me. I had no real clue about guys in general, let alone dating a new one. Between my husband's recent abandonment and the fact I had now been bulimic for nearly thirteen years, I was a mess as far as I was concerned. But I put on a smile and pretended I was just a regular girl. After talking all night, Lance and I discovered we lived only three freeway exits from each other. Before leaving Club Med, we exchanged phone numbers and arranged to meet once home.

Although I was confused and shy, Lance tried his best to break down my walls and get to know me. Several months passed and I was still shocked that someone as good-looking, educated, and athletic as he liked me. I knew one thing for sure, I needed to feel needed. I yearned for the companionship I had never had. When he told me how much he loved me and said I was the perfect girl for him, I was on cloud nine and forgot about my dreary life. I forgot about my hardship and focused only on the fact that Lance had professed his love for me. I didn't care how crazy it was that I was getting involved with someone so soon after Matt left me. I hadn't even cleared my debt, let alone gotten divorced. I filed the papers and at the same time filed for a Catholic annulment. I did this because I thought anyone I met, guy or girl, coworker or boss, might perceive me in a better light. I also thought it might help me go to heaven. According to what I'd learned from the Catholic faith, if I got divorced and especially if I remarried, I'd go to hell. Maybe annulment could save me. Nevertheless, I didn't care about any of that for the moment. I saw only the possibility love offered.

Three months after Lance and I went out on our first date, we were intimate. At twenty-six, I had never been with anyone other than Matt. I didn't think about consequences, but after two weeks I had a fever of a hundred and three. Every inch of my body ached. Every part of my head throbbed. What was going on? Why was my back aching to the point I couldn't get out of bed? What was happening to me? I felt fine yesterday. I wasn't run down, so I couldn't understand why I'd gotten so sick literally overnight. I told Susan. "Jocelyn, I think you might have herpes," she blurted.

"What? That's not possible. I'm not promiscuous. I'm not wild at all. This can't be right. Besides, Lance is a good guy. We waited, I waited to be intimate. He told me he loved me, that I was the perfect girl for him. No way can this be right," I replied. "There's got to be another explanation."

I dragged myself to the local medical facility and as I lay on the cold bed with just a sheer white dressing gown on, the doctor came back into the room. "Jocelyn, I am sorry to tell you but you are very sick. You have contracted herpes. I did a culture and it came up positive."

"Please tell me this isn't true. Please tell me there's a possibility something else is wrong with me. I'm not a bad person. I try to be good," I pleaded. The doctor could do nothing, herpes is incurable. I left the hospital feeling more broken than ever before, like shattered glass. I'm damaged goods, I told myself. I'm unworthy of anything now. I'll never be happy and I'll never be loved. My life is over. No one will touch me with a ten-foot pole now. Damaged goods, Jocelyn, damaged goods. That's all you are now. Go home and be alone. It's just you and your bulimia now.

The years had not helped me overcome my insecurities and debilitating self-doubt, so I believed Lance when he adamantly and angrily stated it wasn't him who gave me herpes, that I must have gotten it elsewhere, perhaps even from Matt. "That's impossible," I told him, "because once someone is in contact with the disease it surfaces in two week, not six months." I was certain, too, that Matt didn't cheat on me. He was too busy getting high.

As the months wore on, I felt completely stripped of my womanhood. I felt cheated I'd had sex with only two people in my life, I hadn't slept around. I thought I was different. Stupid that's all. Jocelyn you are stupid and now you'll pay the price forever, I chastised myself. Because I firmly believed I was damaged goods from every aspect—herpes, breast reduction scars, and bulimia—I dared not rock the boat with Lance. I believed if he left me, I'd be alone forever. If I were a guy, I thought, I wouldn't want me. I wouldn't want to get involved with a basket case like myself. Way too much baggage for someone only twenty-six.

In addition to all this, my relationship with Lance had changed from the blissful early days when he was thoughtful and caring. Now he would often belittle me by telling me how poor I was, that I couldn't afford even the lawn in front of his house. Or that I was fatter than the other girls he worked with, which he announced to me just before we were due to go on his corporate trip to Hawaii. "All the girls are dieting for the trip, Jocelyn, you should too." I was trying. I was trying so hard that I was throwing up everything and then some. Despite feeling inferior all the time, I dared not stand up for myself. If on very rare occasions I did, he somehow twisted it around and made me feel guilty for even bringing up whatever was upsetting me. I couldn't win either way.

When it came to having fun, Lance would do only what he wanted to do. If I had a commitment and invited him along, he'd always act like he wasn't having a good time, complaining on the way home or turning his nose up at the event. It was his way or no way.

"Jocelyn, get a spine," he'd say to me so many times that those words became toxic to me. Didn't he have the slightest idea that I was tired of feeling beaten up by others, that I was sensitive and hurt by his remarks and his unwillingness to be with me at social occasions? Others could see my sadness, why couldn't he? Perhaps he did and just didn't care.

Eventually Lance broke up with me. Four years later I received a letter from him: *Dear Jocelyn … For the last year I've been engaging myself in a group, better known as the Forum. It has helped me in every possible aspect of my life. I have acknowledged who I am not only to myself but to hundreds of people within the Forum. In doing so I am a much better person. I've been working the "program" incessantly. This program has enabled me to be at peace and live a fuller life. I further write to you to concede that I gave you herpes. I played Russian roulette with your health. For that I am sorry. Because this Forum is so amazing, I have included the local chapter in your area for you to consider.... I hope all is well. You can reach me at 555-1212 if you like. Love, Lance.*

I couldn't believe it. I knew it. The bastard. He put me through years of pain and anguish, questioning how I became infected. Four years of agonizing and suffering came down to a couple of trite sentences in what was an advertisement for a cult. There was no real emotion. The letter was so clinical, almost formulaic, but at least I had the truth in black and white for what it was worth to me now. My health would never be the same. I would never be the same. Once again, he was more into himself and now this cult, than truly being sorry for what he did to me.

I turned to my bulimia for solace, hoping to numb, block out, and make all my pain go away. I just couldn't get over the overarching feeling that I was damaged goods, no longer a woman, no longer much of a person. Did God punish me because I was a sinner? Catholicism, the old Catholic guilt so deeply ingrained, lurked in the back of my mind. Crazy as it was, I thought I had gotten herpes as punishment for having sex before my annulment came through. I worried I hadn't been a good enough wife and thought it no wonder Matt had left me. I broke my marriage vows, my sacrament. I broke many sacraments. I convinced myself I was a sinner.

Bulimia was my entire life now. I binged and purged night and day. I'd leave work at lunchtime and race home to binge on whatever was in the kitchen, run upstairs to my bathroom, punish myself by throwing up, and then head back to work as if nothing had happened. I took every kind of "new and improved" diet pill, laxative, suppository, and began regularly using enemas. I ran every day at four thirty in the morning because I spent my evenings working at the retail store. Running became my quality alone time, just me and the pavement below. I'd cry as I ran along the path beside the water, barely able to see what was in front of me in the pre-dawn darkness. I was so familiar with that bike path that I could run it with my eyes closed if I had to. I needed this time. I needed to let out my cries, and I remained hopeful that God would hear me and help me. That he'd forgive me. I hated my life and I hated myself.

Chapter 15

Paying the Price

I ignored the stomach pains that plagued me on and off over the years, considering them simply a by-product of my bulimia, but now something had changed. The pain was beyond anything I'd ever experienced before. I tried everything to alleviate it. Was it my diet, I mean what I actually ate and kept down? Was it lack of sleep? Was it my sadness? Or was it just stress? I didn't have a clue. But everyday the aches seemed to grow worse and more acute. I had been abusing laxatives, suppositories, and enemas for a long time and began to wonder if this could be the reason for my constant throbbing stomach. I needed them, even though I knew I shouldn't be taking them. I was completely dependent on them, and whatever damage was done was done. I couldn't have a bowel movement without the aid of a laxative. If I tried without them, I'd fail and the pain would be tenfold. I was no longer normal. I'd spend nearly two hours every morning in the bathroom, trying to rid myself of my waste. I'd take numerous laxatives the night before so I could relieve myself the next day. Then in the morning, I'd swallow pills, use suppositories, and enemas. I would even lie on the cold bathroom floor, waiting for something to happen.

I couldn't go to work until I had tried to go to the toilet, otherwise the intense pain would make it impossible to concentrate. My head ached, my body was hot and sweaty, and my equilibrium was completely out of whack. The cramping, tightness, and swelling felt like a knife jabbing in and out of my left side. If my attempts at going to the bathroom failed, I would vomit whatever was still undigested in my stomach. This was not self-induced, but an involuntary reaction to my constipation and pain. It was hell.

The various doctors I visited over the course of the next year dismissed my pain. I never told them I was a self-abusive bulimic. While I was losing my battle with the pain, I now faced something much worse and frightening. I was losing complete control of my bowels, not just the occasional time such as when I was in San Diego. Now I'd wake up night after night, drenched in pools of stool, pajamas soiled, bed linens soiled. I felt I'd be better off dead. I was worried and distressed. I can't live like this anymore, I reasoned. I've got to do something. How will I be able to work and support myself if I don't know when diarrhea is going to blast out of me? What do I have to live for now?

Yet another new doctor examined me, gave me numerous tests such as total body x-rays and barium enemas, put me on a liquid diet, and gave me various prescriptions. But nothing cured my pain or changed my condition. Either the food never moved and up it came or it literally fell out my bottom. After many visits back to Stanford Hospital in Palo Alto, the doctor finally gave me some options. "Jocelyn, your large intestines do not seem to be functioning properly. They aren't transporting your food from the small intestines. Consequently, you aren't able to have a normal bowel movement and you experience this pain and distress, what we call colon inertia. The colon no longer works. The only thing I can do for you is elective surgery. Either you can continue to try and live like this, or you can have your large intestines removed."

I took some time to work through what the doctor had told me. Surgery, removal of large intestines. It sounded so drastic, yet how could I live my life like this? Could I? Did I just need to ride this one out? No, I had tried living through it for years in the hope it would dissipate but it continued to grow worse. I knew there wasn't the slightest hope for any semblance of a normal life if something didn't change. I couldn't deal with this condition—how could anyone? Even Susan had a hard time seeing me live like that. It was way too much baggage and distress for anyone, including me.

I agreed to go ahead with the surgery, knowing that not only would my large intestines be removed, but there was the possibility of having to use a colostomy bag either temporarily or for the rest of my life. I decided I couldn't live without having at least some control over my body. As petrified as I was, I knew my many years of laxative, enema, and bulimic abuse had caused me to be like a helpless infant. Literally, I had killed my intestine. It stopped working because I was so desperate to find happiness by being thin. Risk meant little to me. I thought feeling thin and loved was worth taking any chance.

My family did not consult the doctor prior to my surgery. I wasn't a child, but with such major surgery, I wished they'd be more inquisitive. It wasn't until I was in the pre-op room under anesthesia that my dad asked the surgeon, "Should Jocelyn be doing this?"

The surgeon took a hard look at him for a moment. "You're a little too late to be asking that question now, Mr. Bennet."

My mom said and did nothing. She cried to me, but as usual, that was all she did. She put pressure on me by making my illness into something stressful for her. I wanted to scream at her, "Mom, how about showing you care by conferring with my doctor or reading some type of medical information with regard to colon inertia? How about actually taking a real look at me, the daughter who tried to reach out to you and ask for help way back when I was seventeen? I'm twenty-eight now and unless you are so ignorant or in such denial—even Susan knew I was bulimic—you might put two and two together and realize how I got here." I should have expected that she'd be passive as always, never acting in a mature and motherly way. I had to accept I was on my own. I knew it from the start.

The risks were high, not only because the doctors were cutting me open, but because I would need to go under anesthesia. I didn't care. My real concern was the chance I'd have to use a colostomy bag permanently. Even so, with all my surgeon's warnings and with my knowledge that I was the one who caused all this, I knew I had to go through with it. I couldn't go to the bathroom like a normal person, let alone live like one. It would have been impossible for me to maintain any level of sanity if I had to wake up every night covered in my own feces or have an accident at work. I saw no other option. On November 6, 1997 at Stanford Hospital in Palo Alto, I had a total colostomy and my large intestines were removed permanently.

Surgery went exceptionally well and according to my doctor, I was a superb patient. No problems and no complications. The aftermath, however, was a good deal worse than I had expected. The incision ran from my pelvic bone to halfway up my stomach and was far more painful than I'd expected, even with my unlimited supply of morphine. Because the incision cut right through my stomach muscles, it was very difficult to lift myself up or move my body into different positions. I had to have a nurse help me sit up and lie back down, and it was impossible to use the bathroom to relieve myself without a catheter. Despite the tremendous pain and discomfort I was experiencing, emotionally I felt far worse. My bulimia had taken me to such deep, dark places that I had to have part of me removed. Not even the doctors at Stanford could find a remedy to fix me. Would this be the final wake-up call I needed to finally stop or get help?

My family and friends came to visit, trying to cheer up my stay at Stanford. I faked being happy and laughed and joked with them. But their shallow friendships and minimal amount of caring only made me feel lonelier. Couldn't anyone see what was going on with me? I never said anything. It didn't seem to matter and my negative self-talk didn't help either. *Maybe they are all right. I'm Jocelyn, the screwed-up young adult, no different from when I was the screwed-up fat kid in grade school or the screwed-up, makeup-encrusted teen in high school. Unfortunate things happen to people who are not worthy, and I am not worthy.*

Once I was able to regain some of my strength, I began obsessing about my weight. I could tell by feeling my stomach and thighs I had lost weight and that pleased me. But now my mind wandered as I began to contemplate exactly how much weight I had lost permanently by losing my large intestines. I guessed a few pounds and felt overjoyed in a crazy way knowing that I could never regain that weight. Part of my insides were gone and there was no way of getting that back. Those few pounds were gone forever. As I celebrated internally, I also began to once again obsess about the IV and how many calories might be dripping into me. Crazy thoughts, but I couldn't control them.

I was released after one week. I was happy to note I'd weighed one hundred twelve when I went in and now I was one hundred four. Not bad for five feet five inches tall, I thought. In fact, fairly impressive. I hadn't weighed that little in many years. I marveled at feeling thin and focused my energy towards what I needed to do to maintain. I wanted to beat the yo-yo weight thing once and for all, as I'd lost and gained over one hundred pounds over the years. I felt too weak to binge and purge immediately. My appetite hadn't returned entirely yet, so I took advantage and restricted, which I could do with relative ease.

I was determined to make a speedy recovery. The surgeon and my primary care physician had instructed me to wait at least eight weeks before I resumed any rigorous activities, but I couldn't wait that long and in less than a month I was back at the gym. I was entirely focused on my disease and the vicious behaviors that accompanied it. All I cared about was keeping the weigh off and losing more. I was more focused on working out to burn calories than waiting for my abdominal muscles to heal properly. I must have had some serious luck on my side for once because I didn't cause any damage, but it was another measure of the crazy chances I would take with my health just to get and stay thin.

This life-altering event did not prove to be the catalyst for seeking the help I needed. I returned to binging and purging as if nothing ever happened. For a while I stopped taking laxatives and that was a big accomplishment for me. At least I was pain free if only for a short period. The bulimic inside me, however, was too powerful. Not even my dance with death could deter me from indulging in my most violent and abusive acts. Shortly after I returned home from the hospital, and well before I went back to the gym to exercise, I revisited my old behaviors. I drove frantically from shop to shop, eating everything I could in the quest to stuff my feelings deep inside and punish myself for the mess I had now gotten myself into. And doing this enabled me to push away any thoughts of further medical complications my behavior might induce.

Just before I had my surgery, I obtained a job selling software for another Fortune 500 company, a promotion for me. I would be in outside sales and no longer confined to staring at the walls of a small cubicle, dialing for dollars. I was a sales junior. That meant I reported to a senior rep with whom I worked directly, but I was happy knowing I'd be out and about and not stuck inside all day. Best of all, my base salary increased substantially. Now I would have money and be able to live a little, too, as I'd finally gotten myself out from under the debt my ex-husband had left.

One of the main reasons I got the job was because my sister, Susan, worked for the company. She was a great sales rep, one of their best, and always exceeded her quota. After my surgery I started my new job, dismissing whatever abdominal pains I continued to have. I worked long hours trying to impress my boss, which was more important than the stabbing pains that had returned. Even working hard didn't stop or slow down my bulimic behaviors, though. I readjusted my schedule accordingly. I'd exercise mostly in the very early hours of the morning, binge sometimes before work but always after, and attempt to restrict my food intake while at work. It was impossible for me to eat without throwing up, so I had to micro-manage my food when I didn't have the opportunity to eliminate whatever I ate. Susan was an independent sales rep, so she scheduled her time differently than I did and usually arrived home an hour or so after me. This gave me the freedom and opportunity to get in a quick binge and purge session. Later, when Susan was at the gym, I'd embark on a much bigger and more violent episode, usually driving to local fast-food restaurants, bringing home bags of greasy fried food, shoving it down my throat, and running upstairs to be alone in my bathroom. If that binge wasn't enough to relieve me from whatever emotion I was trying to bury, I'd engage in another smaller binge later. By ten o'clock, I was so exhausted I'd fall into bed and go straight to sleep.

The fiscal year was passing and my big sales were not coming in. I was working as hard as I could, but able to bring in only smaller deals. As expected, my boss was losing faith and increasingly put pressure on me to make something happen. How was I to make it all happen? Why wasn't he pulling in any revenue? I went on more calls than he did. And I actually made a few sales, unlike him. He was my boss so I couldn't say the things I wanted to. I did what he said because I needed my job and liked the company, despite the deterioration of my relationship with him.

Instead of working as a team, we grew further apart over time. I recoiled from him and he, too, drew back. Soon his offhand remarks turned uglier and then gave way to nasty e-mails. I couldn't pull a miracle out of nowhere. Hard as I tried, I wasn't succeeding. I knew in sales it mattered little whether you tried hard or put in long hours. What mattered were the sales, the bottom line.

I became increasingly unhappy and resentful and focused inward on my bulimia. I'd always wanted to be a good worker and was embarrassed at not driving in enough revenue. I began to work from home so I could find relief by binging during the day. Or I'd schedule appointments at specific times, so I could do a mini drive-by. I sought solace, comfort, and self-punishment through food, knowing I was playing a potentially lethal game with my health.

The following year, I was promoted to a position with responsibility for my own territory. My boss recognized he had treated me appallingly and put in a good word for me so I'd get the promotion. Maybe he was trying to say he was sorry. I'll never know, but in any event, I was grateful. Adding to the immense pride and happiness I felt was the bonus that I was moving. My new territory covered part of Southern California, so at the end of 1998, I loaded up my Jeep Wrangler and headed to sunny Santa Monica.

My apartment was cute, all bright and white with lots of sun shining through every window, just the way I liked things to be. It was only a one bedroom and I was going to have to work from home, but I didn't mind. The company I was working for wouldn't allow me to have my own office until I proved myself worthy of one by reaching my sales quota. I bought a cheap plywood desk and set up an office in the corner of the family room. I would be confined to my little apartment unless I was seeing a customer. I didn't care. I no longer had to get up at four thirty to go for a run. Nor did I have to sit in bumper-to-bumper traffic morning and evening. And I was so happy not to have to deal with my boss breathing down my neck.

My new position brought new challenges. First, I knew no one in Santa Monica, let alone in the Los Angeles area. I knew meeting people would be very difficult. I was insecure and shy and because I worried constantly about being bulimic and too fat, where would I ever meet anyone should I want to? Still, I was away from Northern California and for that I was very happy.

Having my own territory and being responsible for $1.2 million in sales was going to be a big challenge. I was willing and thankful for the opportunity and didn't care that I'd be working long hours during the week and some on the weekends. Shortly after I settled into my apartment and became familiar with my new territory, I learned how crummy it was and how difficult it would be for me to reach my quota. Even with that knowledge, I was excited about selling out in the field and felt fortunate to have this opportunity. I was ready to give it my best shot.

Several months passed and by working nonstop, I discovered a potentially lucrative sales deal. Because of the nature of the company and possible revenue, I had my boss join me on the sales call. I didn't want to screw it up and knew if I was successful I'd not only make my annual quota, but also I'd be seen as a winner. My boss also thought it would be a good opportunity to bring along the newest member of the company to help him get up to speed.

On Thursday morning at ten, we all sat in what I thought to be the Blue Cross reception area. "Jocelyn and team, you can come in now," the lady at the desk called out. Carrying our laptops and with handouts to distribute, we filed into the meeting room. Once all the "Blue Cross" attendees were present, I began to move forward with my presentation. "Stop," Jack, VP of IT, cried out, "we are not Blue Cross. Don't you have any idea where you are? This is Wellpoint. We are a direct competitor to Blue Cross." He was furious. On what now seemed to be the biggest overhead screen in the world, I had inserted on nearly every slide of my presentation the name Blue Cross in big bold letters. I wanted to die right then and there. Then Jack abruptly stood up and began to walk out of the room.

I was so embarrassed. I couldn't believe I'd made such a huge mistake. Didn't I see the sign that loomed on top of the building we'd just entered? I turned bright red while sweat pored down my face, back, and underarms. I blurted out I was terribly sorry for the mistake. Jack could tell my apology was genuine, not to mention he could see how humiliated, embarrassed, and ashamed I felt. He offered to give me another chance.

After what seemed to be the most awkward and stressful meeting ever—even my boss was dumbfounded, let alone the new guy—the meeting finally came to an end. I'm sure it is safe to say that everyone was as glad as I was when it was over. Jerry, my boss, never expressed anger towards me and, without exchanging any words, he knew how horrible I felt. Jack moved along with his recommendations as far as what he wanted me to do for the next steps, and we went our separate ways. I knew I had let everyone down. I couldn't wait to drive off and cry. All I could think of was my need to binge and purge right then.

I cried and berated myself as I drove. "Jocelyn, how could you screw up so badly? You made a fool of yourself and the company. It's inexcusable. You're never going to succeed. You're a loser."

I knew I needed to punish myself for causing such a mess. I couldn't handle feeling all the emotions I had. I needed to stuff them away, numb myself. Where would I go? Where could I stop? McDonald's was just off the freeway to the right. I'd go there first. "May I have a number three and a number seven? I will also need a large order of onion rings, an apple pie, and a chocolate shake," I said, pretending I was getting food for someone else too. Then, as I consumed the hamburgers, chicken sandwich, fries, and onion rings while driving recklessly, I planned my next destination. Burger King was on Wilshire, I could stop off there, get another big combo meal, and finish by going to Jack in the Box on Twenty-Sixth Street. I'd bring home the Jack in the Box food and whatever Burger King I didn't finish.

I sat at my kitchen table with all the blinds closed so none of my neighbors could see me shoving bite after bite into my mouth. I didn't taste or even feel the many different textures of the food. I concentrated only on eating everything in front of me as fast as possible. Tears were still streaming down my face. I barely chewed the food, practically swallowing it whole. I couldn't let go of what just happened or the feeling I had once again failed. I failed myself, my boss, and Wellpoint.

Finally, when I couldn't eat another bite, I headed off to my bathroom and, like so many times in the past, I knew that I'd eaten far too much to throw up in the toilet. I might cause a back up and what if I couldn't fix it and needed to call the landlord? Too big a chance, I couldn't take the risk. I took a plastic trash bag, placed it into my trash bin, and threw up in that. Minutes passed as food continued to come up and out. Once it was all over, I carried it to the bin outside. A few feet from the dumpster, the bag suddenly broke and my purge gushed out the bottom. I looked up and saw a man standing nearby. Disgust spread across his face as shame spread across mine. Panicking, I tried to shove my purge back into the bag with my bare hands. Whatever I couldn't fit into the broken bag, I moved to the side of the pavement. I was mortified. What did this man think of me? Surely he knew it was vomit. How could he not? Without looking up at his face again, I made a run for my apartment.

Jocelyn, certainly that will empower you to stop binging. You just humiliated yourself beyond your wildest dreams. You were bringing your own throw-up to the dumpster and scooping it up with your bare hands, in public. You are completely mad. I knew in my heart, though, I couldn't stop. I couldn't just tell myself enough was enough, no more bulimia. I was so deep into my disease that even the most humiliating situation could not help me stop.

It was now the fall of 1999. It had been two years since I'd had my large intestines removed. Even after such radical surgery, I still hadn't been able to arrest my disorder and go without binging and purging regularly. I refused to think about the pressures it be having on my now weakened, incomplete body and continued to eat every kind of binge food I craved.

Towards the end of that year, I woke one evening with unbearable stomach pains. I tried to dismiss them, blaming an upset stomach from binging and purging too hard. And then I'd taken a variety of diet pills, too. Thinking that's probably what it was, I self-medicated by taking every kind of pain medicine I could buy at the local drugstore. Days went by, but I felt no relief from the intensifying pain. A friend whom I'd met just a short time ago gave me a special curing herb she smuggled in illegally from Bolivia. This herb was supposed to do magic and get rid of even the worst ailments but, unfortunately, not even that worked to overcome my pain.

I endured nearly a week of this intense stomachache until one evening I discovered I looked pregnant—my stomach was fully extended, like a second trimester mother-to-be. I knew something was very wrong with me at this point because I certainly wasn't pregnant. It would have to have been by Immaculate Conception as I wasn't dating anyone, let alone having sex. I crawled out of bed at two in the morning, terribly frightened, and walked to Santa Monica/UCLA hospital wearing a sweat suit and carrying only my wallet and apartment key. I was admitted into emergency where they did all kinds of tests. Early the following morning, the doctor told me an orange-sized ovarian cyst had ruptured, producing internal pain and bleeding. Worse, I had an obstruction on my intestine. He indicated the obstruction was positioned on the original suture of my first surgery, where my small intestines were reconnected to my stomach. I needed to have two distinctive surgeries, the first with a gynecological surgeon to remove the remaining cyst and its debris and the second with a gastrointestinal surgeon to fix my obstruction.

I knew all of this was the result of my continued hard-core bulimia, but again I mentioned none of this to the doctors. Prior to admitting me into the operating room, I had to have my gastrointestinal system cleaned out with a stomach pump to avoid complications during surgery. I hadn't had a bowel movement in a week, despite all the laxatives, enemas, and suppositories I'd used, so I figured I must be pretty backed up. I thought okay, no big deal, it will be over before I know it and that will be that. Was I wrong.

For several months I had been on a very restrictive vegetable diet when I wasn't binging and purging and unbeknownst to me, my body was full of undigested vegetables. The doctors at Stanford never mentioned any particular foods I needed to avoid, but apparently some vegetables were a not a good idea for me. To get them out, a tube ran down my throat into my stomach where it remained for six days pumping buckets of food, broccoli in particular. I couldn't believe how painful this was or that I was actually capable of storing so much food in the first place. I only weighed one hundred twelve pounds. By the end of the sixth day, my throat hurt so badly it surpassed the pain I felt in my abdomen. Once there was nothing left to pump out, I was given the green light and rolled away to surgery.

By now both my parents and Susan had come down. Susan came and went but because she was more responsible than my parents, she took action and asked the doctors all the necessary questions I was remiss in asking. She also took care of all my unfinished business at work, writing e-mails, calling my customers, and the like, before she returned home. My parents were useless. They didn't do anything other than the menial—they cleaned my apartment and bought me a few needed household items. My mom acted sicker than I did in front of everyone, so much so that once she left, one of my surgeons asked me if she was okay. *Is my mom okay? Yes, she's okay. In fact that's my mom as I know her, unable to handle anything without acting like a mental patient herself. It's always all about her. Anything significant in my life somehow turns around and upsets her. I end up consoling her and ignoring myself.*

I was embarrassed and saddened by the doctor's question. In sixty-eight years my mom had not learned an appropriate reaction to any difficult situation. And my dad, he did nothing, mostly watched TV in my room. So I underwent both surgeries, one after the other, with a successful outcome and still feeling utterly alone.

Unlike the first, the pain I felt this time was beyond intense. I felt like a knife was being plunged deep into my side. The agony was unbearable. Although the surgery went well, I personally wasn't doing so well, and spent the next three days in ICU. I lay alone in a cold room with an epidural in my back to try and help alleviate my pain. I was too sick and weak to have visitors. During that time, a priest came and said the last rites. It was not certain I would make it this time. Did I mess up so badly I was going to die? Was my bulimia going to finally get me?

I didn't know, but something inside me told me to hang on—for what I didn't know at the time. I did know I was terribly sick and while part of me was sad, another part cared little. I was so engulfed in my disease that nothing brightened my spirits. My job? No. It was a lot of pressure for little reward. My usual day of binge and purge, binge and purge? No, it was like a violent roller coaster I couldn't get off. The priest, though, was more compassionate than my mom and dad ever were or even any of the priests I had known back in Catholic school. He seemed to look right into my heart and willed me to live. It worked. After my three-day stay in the ICU, I was released and returned to a regular room on the fourth floor. With an IV in my arm and a button nearby to push anytime I desired morphine, I wondered if I would ever be pain free again.

By the tenth day in the hospital, I was feeling dirty, disgusting, and hungry. I'd not had a single bite of food since I'd gotten there and was allowed only lemon-flavored q-tips, which I could suck on but that did hardly anything to satisfy my hunger pangs. I started getting delirious as my hunger grew. I wished I could binge and purge. In total, I spent thirteen days in the Santa Monica/UCLA hospital and as I left, I again contemplated whether my second dance with death would finally change something. Bulimia was such a strong and seductive addiction that the answer would again be no.

Unlike the last time I was in the hospital, I was advised by my physician and later a nutritionist that I'd have to change my diet completely. How? If I wasn't binging and purging, I certainly knew I wasn't eating greasy and unhealthy foods. I was eating vegetables, lots of them, protein and fruit too. How could this be wrong? I could recite the nutritional contents of nearly every food available. I'd had years of practice. It turned out these types of foods were precisely the wrong ones for me. How ironic that the healthy foods were the ones killing me. When I had my large intestines removed, someone had neglected to inform me that my body was no longer able to digest and process fibrous and cellulous foods such as vegetables, fruits, and even grains, the way a normal person's body can. They took a very long time to pass through me and sometimes they simply couldn't. The nutritionist told me I more or less had to follow a life-long diet, one of bland, mostly tasteless foods. "Like a person with Crohn's disease, Jocelyn, you will have to follow a low-residue diet from now on," she said.

"Great, I'm twenty-nine and have just been put on another diet." I felt like I was back in school with my mom putting me on one weight loss program after another. The nutritionist sounded to me a lot like the old Diet Center lady.

"You are allowed only the foods on the list and no others." Her approach was Nutrition 101, with plastic food to represent portion sizes. She gave me a few brochures on types of food I could eat such as chicken, consommé, oatmeal, etc. and a pyramid of food groups. I already knew everything she told me. I never returned, feeling I'd wasted a hundred fifty dollars.

Once I accepted this new way of eating I found, much to my surprise, the biggest challenge was not the diet, but the embarrassment I experienced when I was in a situation that required me to eat in the company of others. It was difficult having to explain why I was eating, for example, no vegetables or salad and plain chicken with no sauce because it might have garlic, onions, or too many spices, etc. I'd regularly get strange looks, as if I were half telling the truth or that I was some high-maintenance freak who would eat only certain foods. Yes, I was bulimic and fanatic, but I didn't care to announce it to the world and had, thus far, done my best to hide it from everyone.

Being on a restricted diet was difficult to explain without going into detail. It wasn't that easy for others to grasp. I'd tell people I had stomach surgery and this was how I had to eat. But often that failed to satisfy and they'd start to interrogate me, which made me uneasy. I'd squirm, and they'd give me a look of confusion or disbelief. I'd try to blow them off and change the subject. I couldn't say, "Gee I got this way because I'm bulimic and, by the way, I abused laxatives and diet pills, so I no longer have my large intestines. What little I have left is so fragile I couldn't eat like a normal person even if I wanted to."

I lived with the consequences every day of what I'd done to myself. Being bulimic had forever changed my life. I didn't need to tell people my private business. In the end, there was no answer that successfully put closure to the awkward situation, and I started to loathe going out to eat—I'd stress about it for days in advance.

None of my most embarrassing situations ever helped me overcome my compulsive behaviors. It didn't matter that the stranger in the alley looked sickened by the throw-up he witnessed spilling out of my plastic bag. It didn't matter that I had my large intestines removed at twenty-seven because I destroyed myself to the point I was like an infant who couldn't control her bowels. It didn't matter that I had an obstruction caused by my continuation of bulimia and had to undergo surgery again or that a priest had administered the last rites to me.

Nothing seemed to empower me enough to stop. I resigned myself to being bulimic for the rest of my life. I would cheat whenever I could and not follow my diet. I already knew I would binge and purge as soon as I could. And all bets were off as far as food choices. I knew I'd devour everything I wasn't supposed to eat, then throw up. This new diet made me feel like the young me being put on one diet after another. Again, someone was telling me what I could and couldn't eat. It didn't matter. I'd follow my own rules just like my inner bulimic me, and hope for the best.

PART III
THE REDEMPTION

Chapter 16

Out from the Shadows

In January 2000, as in previous years, all the sales reps from the company—500 or so including some of the product development team—met at an off site location for a sales kickoff event. I flew to Arizona where I would learn about all the new products soon to be released, view live demonstrations, and attend dinners and parties. By now I felt relatively comfortable going to these functions, and I knew enough people to talk with to get through an event.

I hadn't fully recovered from my surgery in November, probably because I was throwing up less than two weeks after. I wasn't at the top of my game, so I didn't prepare as thoroughly as I usually would have for such an event. I loved clothes and would hyper-obsess about what to wear but I wasn't in the best frame of mind. I hadn't impressed anyone so far and presumed I wasn't going to now. I more or less shoved whatever work appropriate pieces I had into my suitcase the night before and settled with that.

The first several days were just like previous kickoff meetings. There were product meetings all day long followed by dinner, usually between six thirty and eight thirty. Then after dinner there would be some type of entertainment. Typically, I'd bail out of dinner, go to my room, eat a Met-Rx bar, and binge on all the food in the refrigerator, then head for the toilet. Should the dinner be mandatory attendance, I'd pick at the food and excuse myself by saying I wasn't hungry or I had a big lunch. Nobody took much notice of my eating. While they were consumed with enjoying themselves, I was secretly obsessing about how many calories were in this food or that food. I rarely went to the after-dinner functions. If I did, I'd leave before ten. I didn't feel comfortable in large crowds and preferred to keep my socializing with any coworkers to a minimum.

The week finally ended, and I couldn't wait to go home to my little apartment back in Santa Monica. I was reaching my breaking point in terms of stress. For bulimics like me, lack of control over my schedule, especially regarding food and exercise, was very difficult to handle for more than a few days. I needed to get back to my routine, rituals, and comfort zone. I packed my bags early that day so I could simply come back to the room after the awards banquet in the evening, go to sleep, and wake up fully prepared to fly back to Los Angeles.

That night I chose silver pants, a silver tank top, and silver and black shoes to wear to the banquet. Not bad, I thought, seeing as I hadn't splurged on a new outfit. I might have been a little under-dressed than most of the girls that night, but I didn't care. As usual I picked at my food during dinner, opting to drink the wine instead. Awards were given out to the top sales reps and achievers. The CEO and VPs made speeches and all in all it was a nice, very tastefully done evening. After the formalities ended, everyone went to the bars, the lounges, and the hallways to drink and talk. I joined them and was having a pretty good time. Around two in the morning I decided to call it a night and headed back to my room. As I was making my way through the lobby, Sue, an acquaintance, approached and asked me if I'd join her for the after-hours party. Without giving it a second thought, I surprised myself by agreeing. I had never gone to an after-hours party before. As we entered the suite, the festivities were in full swing.

Sue didn't stick around. She found a cute guy to talk to and left me standing in the middle of the large suite, surrounded by nearly forty or so Irish people from the company's Dublin, Ireland development center. I didn't know anyone and was feeling increasingly timid. Should I leave? Should I stay? What should I do? Then I made the most out-of-character decision in my life up to that point. I had secretly fancied one particular Irish guy, although I never so much as exchanged a hello with him. When I noticed him at the party, I had a strong urge to talk to him. For the first time ever, I acted spontaneously, not giving the voices in my head time to talk me out of it. I tapped him on the back and as he turned around I said, "Hi, my name is Jocelyn. Would you please stop drinking so you can get to know me sober?"

What did I just do? Was I crazy? I couldn't take back my words. Would he tell me to go away, think I was a nut for even asking him that? He placed his beer on the adjacent table and said, "Sure." I knew right then that something magical had just occurred. I forgot how shy and timid I was. My focus was completely on the two of us. Immediately we were laughing and enjoying ourselves. John was like no one I had spoken to in my life. Who was this guy, and why did I feel I didn't want to stop talking to him ever? I couldn't make sense of my thoughts. It didn't matter because either way, I was looking forward to the ride.

For the next nine and a half months John and I commuted back and forth each weekend, alternating between San Francisco, where he lived, and Santa Monica so we could spend time with each other. In between our weekend visits, we'd talk on the phone for hours every night. By talking incessantly we got to know each other very well. We talked about everything imaginable, except my history with bulimia. I was happy. I was in love. And I seemed to have fewer days with a bulimic episode. I was so excited to be with John, I wasn't as consumed with my disease. I felt wonderful. How nice it was to have something more important to concentrate on. Deep down I knew I wasn't miraculously cured just because I was in love, but still I knew I could always rely on my expertise in hiding my bulimia when it reawakened.

From the moment I tapped John on the back, I knew in my heart he was special, magical. The kindness and warmth he possessed was unsurpassed by anyone I had ever known. He was smart and witty, and how lucky I was he loved me. We spent our time together playing tennis, reading, going to nightclubs, traveling, and anything and everything we could think of. He was my first real and genuine best friend.

John was the first and only person who continued to tell me he loved me for me, for what was inside. He's crazy, I thought. In love, yes, but crazy. How can he see my inside and still love me? I don't even love myself. I worried that one day he'd wake up and discover me to be the complete dysfunctional basket case I felt I was, but he never did. I waited and waited, but he continued to see my true self and not the person I always believed everyone else saw. After dating just three months, John asked me to marry him while we were vacationing in Hawaii. I couldn't say yes quickly enough.

On November 17, 2000 John and I were married at St. Monica's church in Santa Monica. We had a very small, intimate wedding with only our parents attending and then a lovely dinner in the Polo Lounge of the Beverly Hills Hotel where we were staying. It was special for both of us, and we were glad we chose not to have a big, elaborate wedding. This was our day and magical it was.

Since John was doing exceptionally well at work and I was growing tired of my job, we agreed it was best I move up north, rather than he look for another position in Los Angeles. Together we drove my Jeep Wrangler packed high with all my belongings to 3265 Diamond Heights Boulevard, San Francisco. I was officially Mrs. John Golden. We were happy together. We got along fantastically.

After we settled into the apartment John found, I discovered even the change of scenery did little to abate my bulimic behaviors. Although early in our dating my bulimia receded, I resumed my binging and purging on a daily basis soon after we moved. I had no reason why. I should have been the happiest person in the world and not eating everything in sight, throwing it all up, and rushing off to the store to replenish the food supply before John got home. The guiltier I felt, the worse my bulimia became. I couldn't stop the vicious cycle. All the promises I made to myself and all the crazy diets I tried just to stop me from throwing up proved unsuccessful. Tomorrow, I'd always say to myself. Tomorrow I will stop. I have to before John finds out. I have to. Tomorrow never came and I never stopped. I seemed to be getting worse.

"A lovely house," Lesley, our real estate agent, commented. "A perfect floor plan in a highly desirable neighborhood." It was love at first sight. Small, quaint, like a doll house, I wanted to show it to John immediately. Three bedrooms, two baths, and a yard big enough for a dog, something I'd wanted for as long as I could remember. John loved it too. Within a few months of arriving in San Francisco, we moved into our new home at 202 Blackstone Drive in Danville, in the East Bay.

Things didn't change for me despite having a wonderful husband and beautiful new home. I was feeling down and falling deeper into the grips of my bulimia. John couldn't miss that I avoided certain foods and ate rather strangely. He believed the excuses I gave him—my surgery, can't eat this and that, need to only have this, my stomach hurts, and whatever else was on my list of stock excuses. But his suspicion grew.

We were sitting on our sofa one night after dinner shortly after moving in, when I excused myself saying my stomach hurt and I needed to use the bathroom. I returned over a half hour later. Without hesitating, John turned to me, looking as if he might cry. "You were throwing up, Jocelyn, weren't you?" I felt the blood rush to my face, my body was completely gripped with anxiety. "Jocelyn, I think I've known this for a very long time, I just didn't want to believe it. But I can't deny it any longer."

I knew at that moment I had to be honest. This was the first time I'd felt that way. "Yes, John, I was throwing up." Tears ran down my face and I could barely breathe.

"Why Jocelyn?" he replied almost in a whisper.

"John, I know I should have told you. I know you may never forgive me for being dishonest. I know you may choose to leave me, you might not want to be married to me anymore, but I'm bulimic. I have been so since I was thirteen. I can't stop. I've tried and tried. But I just can't stop." John held me as I rocked back and forth like a little girl, sobbing, my body shaking.

John didn't leave me or didn't turn his back on me. Instead, he reached out to me. He said he'd do anything it took to get me better. That he'd never let me down. He would never give up on me. Never. He wasn't going to let me die from this disease. He loved me for me, the person on the inside, the one only he saw, not the one I saw. Finally I would be forced and supported to get the help I'd needed since that first moment in the bushes so many years before.

I first tried group meetings. Although they were a great means of support, they weren't enough for me and I wasn't able to stop my daily rituals. I put aside the meetings for the time being and made my first call to a professional therapist. As scared as I was, I knew I had to do this, not only for me but for John as well.

Chapter 17

Finding a Therapist

I first began my search for a therapist by calling the ones my health insurance plan covered. I dialed number after number, getting nothing but answering machines. I left a message on each one. To my surprise, not one therapist called me back. Why? I couldn't figure it out. I phoned eleven different ones and no one had the decency or professionalism to follow up with a phone call. Reviewing the messages I had written down so I could speak clearly and not forget to include some relevant information, I withdrew into my negative self and thought I must be too messed up for them to even want to help me.

John was dumbfounded, too, but encouraged me to continue calling. This time I would call therapists who were not covered by my health plan. One after another, I did the same, dialing and leaving messages. Again, no one phoned me back. After calling and leaving one to three messages on twenty-nine answering machines, I connected finally with Carey. She told me to come in and we met the following Tuesday. The first visit with her seemed fairly routine: Tell me a little about yourself, your background, your length of time struggling with bulimia. Nothing too out of the ordinary.

I thought this might work and looked forward to our next meeting the following Tuesday. Promptly at noon I waited in the sitting room until she signaled me to come in. "Jocelyn, have a seat," she said. "I'd like to start by taking you through a personality test." I answered her questions as best I could. One by one Carey read them off checking whatever box corresponded to my remarks. Strange I thought. Surely she can get to know me just by asking me questions rather than using some stupid survey. Besides I was there to talk about my battle with bulimia, not answer questions such as "do you sleep well at night." But since she was the therapist, I figured she knew what she was doing. The session came to a close without my talking about why I was there in the first place. Maybe next time, I thought.

Our third and what was to be final session, Carey was much cooler than before. I sat down, deciding I should just come out and tell her I needed to focus on understanding and recovering from my bulimia. I felt sad confiding in someone my struggle and need for help and tears started running down my cheeks. Carey reacted in a manner I couldn't understand. "Jocelyn, if you are going to cry than I suggest you don't wear eye makeup." What? Why was she putting me down for expressing my feelings and asking for help? What did wearing eye makeup have to do with divulging my struggle with my disease? Her behavior was cold and mean and I felt the room temperature drop. I knew right then that Carey wasn't the person to open up to, especially if this was her first reaction to my sharing part of myself. Then to my complete surprise, she interjected by saying, "I don't actually treat people with eating disorders. That is not my area of expertise."

I couldn't believe it. Why didn't she tell me in the first place? Why did she even agree to meet with me? Why did she waste my time and hers? Money was the only reason that came to mind. She made a quick five hundred dollars off me. Now she proceeded to give me the name and number of a specialist in eating disorders. Angry, I took the little piece of paper from her and walked out the door, never to see her again.

I know, like me, John felt discouraged by this whole ordeal. He was trying to be as supportive as he could, emotionally and financially, but everything I tried seemed to be a dead end. I felt worse about myself after my encounter with Carey. Although I just wanted to quit my search for help, I reluctantly made the call to the therapist on the little piece of scratch paper Carey gave me. Thankfully, Sarah returned my call right away and seemed genuinely kind and welcoming. She had been in private practice treating patients with eating disorders for fourteen years. I was very hopeful.

Our first meeting went wonderfully. Sarah was everything I could imagine in a therapist—warm, sincere, encouraging, supportive, and much more that is almost impossible for me to describe. I felt I had finally come home. I knew immediately I need not look any further. Something was magical about her. I'd found the right person to help me.

Sarah could see I needed a lot of help and together we embarked on a process of intensive psychotherapy counseling. During my twenty-year relationship with bulimia, I had never come close to recovery, despite my many attempts, substituting one obsessive-compulsive behavior with another. This would be a long and arduous journey, one that would take far longer than I imagined. Sarah worked endless hours with me to help me understand the seeds of my bulimia, my inner emptiness, uncovering for me the underlying, unconscious causes of distress that had affected me in my formative years and carried over into my adult years. We explored my memories, feelings, buried experiences, and self-beliefs both past and present.

Sarah worked with me at my deepest emotional level, using tools such as art therapy and hypnotherapy. For the first time in my life I felt I understood why I became bulimic and, a surprise to me, how bulimia had helped me survive. I came to understand my eating disorder encompassed many facets I wasn't aware of such as disturbed family relationships, low self-esteem, intense fear of rejection, abandonment, guilt, conflict resolution, unworthiness, suppressed anger, suppressed creativity, stereotyped beliefs about appropriate appearance and social influences. I buried all these and more by shoving food down my throat. I hadn't allowed myself to recognize feelings or deal with any of these things as they happened. I did not have the tools to understand and successfully work through the challenging circumstances in my life. My way of coping with any of these or any other events was to turn to bulimia.

Prior to meeting with Sarah, I had never explored my feelings and or tried to understand why I felt the way I did or did the things I did. I had never reflected on my childhood and adulthood from any perspective other than I deserved whatever happened to me, that I was unworthy, and that was life. Through my ingrained belief system, I replicated what was happening to me on the outside by administering self-punishment. I never understood that a feeling is just that, a feeling. It's not right or wrong, it just is. For the very first time, I realized the feelings I had about my experiences were valid, that instead of expressing them in a constructive and helpful manner, I had always buried them inside. Little by little these feelings of invisibility, worthlessness, and being too fat to be loved had manifested in the form of bulimia. For the first time, I was given an opportunity to be heard and genuinely cared for. I was learning to be me.

While working out at the gym, a woman in one of my support groups fell off the Stairmaster and simply dropped dead. Her body had given up. I knew all along I, too, was killing myself from the inside out. All through my teens and young adulthood, I hadn't cared if bulimia killed me. I had no hope. But Sarah made me believe in myself and gave me the tools to embrace life in a different fashion.

Sarah wasn't the only therapist I met with regularly. Determined to help me, she recommended I see three additional therapists, each specializing in a certain aspect of bulimia. Without question, John had no fundamental understanding of bulimia let alone how to coexist with someone suffering from it. He gladly accompanied me to one session a week with Ashley, a wonderful therapist. These weekly meetings were critical to John's coming to understand me and my battle, which was crucial to my recovery. He soon learned bulimia is not about vanity, a misconception many people have, but rather it consists of three components, emotional, psychological, and physical. He soon understood that those suffering don't just wake up one day and decide to have an eating disorder, just like someone doesn't wake up and decide they are going to have cancer. Through our weekly sessions, John began to fully understand that bulimia is a way of coping and surviving in a chaotic and dysfunctional environment, within the family and the world outside. He learned it would take a long time to undo all the negative feelings and experiences I carried, while at the same time dismantling my former life and trying to build an entirely new one. It was a hard journey for John and one that took great courage.

Throughout our time spent with Ashley, as we tried to sort out what bulimia meant for me and for both of us as a married couple, John also researched and read about sufferers with bulimia. He committed to working as hard as he had to and for as long as he needed to fully understand and help me. He demonstrated the most precious gift a human can posses, the gift of unconditional and selfless love. This level of love and support from him played a significant role in my journey to recovery. I knew I couldn't turn my back on this miracle. I had to forge ahead.

Although John, Sarah, Ashley, and my other therapists supported me, I still had a long road ahead. I learned that emotionally I was still a teenager because bulimia tends to stunt developmental growth at the emotional level the individual is when he or she is first consumed by the disease. To uncover, understand, unlearn, and re-learn an entirely new way of living was difficult. But the willingness and hope I now had allowed me to start my journey and to start learning to be me, Jocelyn, alone and without my longest companion, my bulimic me.

To the world outside it appeared I had a relaxing life as a non-working wife, but in reality, I was spending four days a week in therapy working harder than I ever had in my life to recover from the grips of my monstrous disease. I immersed myself into individual, group, and shared treatment sessions with John. They all provided tools and support in many different ways.

Let me share with you some of the tools and processes I found most helpful in the hope they may prove useful to you or someone you love. Using different combinations of these tools helped me through different periods of my recovery.

If you are a sufferer, I strongly encourage you to work with your therapist to decide what is best for you.

INDIVIDUAL THERAPY

What	How
Open and supportive discussion	I was allowed to freely share my feelings and emotions without judgment or consequence. I discovered and uncovered my buried experiences, emotions, and feelings while my therapist responded with thoughtful and supportive words and suggestions. For example, I'd always thought I deserved getting herpes because my upbringing had instilled in me that divorce and sex outside of marriage was a serious sin. I believed God punished me with herpes because I was engaging in wrongdoing. My thinking was that of a teen. My therapist's choice words consoled the inner child in me and provided support and alternatives for my crazy conclusions. She provided a sense of calm and enabled me to think differently.
Role-playing	Through creative visualization and meditation, my therapist had me envision having a different mother. For example, I came home from the second grade appearing as if something was upsetting me. Because my mom was so in tune with me, she recognized my state immediately. She gently questioned me until I was comfortable enough to share what was troubling me. Then with positive reassurance, my new mother helped me work through my troubles and resolve my problems with love, kindness, and total support.
Affirmation	Receiving it from others and giving to myself.
Relaxation/meditation, including Chakra	Therapist created tapes for me to use at home.
Unlearning negative self-talk	Unlearn negative reactions, judgments, and feelings and learn positive ones, e.g., replace "I am not worthy" with "I am a worthy person," etc. Use positive affirmation.
Drawing pictures or representations and discussing the meaning	For example, I drew a huge torso with tiny hands and feet. My therapist pointed out that my feet represented balance and my hands represented touching life, both of which I had reduced to nothing and had drawn on a big torso that represented the huge void where I focused all my feelings and thoughts about myself.

INDIVIDUAL THERAPY

What	*How*
Playing with figurines representative of parents, meanings, reasoning, alternatives	My therapist would tell me, for example, to quickly and without thinking pick three figures that represented my mother. This would allow my psyche to be free to act spontaneously and not become compromised by fear of consequences. We would then explore together what we thought the choices represented. For example, I chose a bird, which meant I wanted my mother to fly away, to separate, to leave me alone.
Regression analysis	My therapist had me go back to when, at seventeen, I told my mother I was bulimic, but create a different mother and play out a scenario where my "new" mom embraced me and told me she loved me and would do anything to help me get better. I had to imagine this constantly to overcome and erase the pain of the real rejection.
Understanding appeasement does not allow expression of authentic self	I sacrificed my well-being to keep peace with my parents and appeased them to avoid the feelings of total rejection, disapproval, and separation I thought would follow if I stood up for myself. In doing this, I buried my authentic self and stuffed these feelings by binging on food and then released them by purging. By changing my appeasing behavior, I was able to increase my tolerance for emotional separation and use avenues of expression other than bulimia.
Understanding depression	Until I was able to communicate my feelings and emotions in a constructive way, I wasn't able to heal. Turning my unwanted feelings inward and against myself created a fertile environment for my depression. Through therapy and expression, I rid myself of these feelings and depression.
Feeling and letting go of grief	Unresolved grief preys on emotions and debilitates. I came to realize through one-on-one therapy that my feelings of grief were valid. From that point I was able to truly feel them, work through my feelings, and let go. As a continuing part of my therapy, I talk, share, and cry over my pain rather than turn it inward to self-abuse through bulimia.

INDIVIDUAL THERAPY

What	How
Understanding choices	Because I felt unaccepted and unacceptable, I chose isolation over socialization. Through therapy, I began to build my self-esteem and reach outward by attending such things as the CASA program, group therapy, art classes, etc. This took a great deal of courage, and gentleness, guidance, and encouragement from my therapist. I had to allow myself to be vulnerable and face rejection but the more I practiced this, the less fearful and more adult I became. I came to realize I had many options to use other than bulimia. For example, instead of purging my feelings destructively, I write, talk to John, go for a walk, take a bath, go for a drive, etc.
Understanding fears	By openly and honestly communicating my fears with my therapist, she was able to encourage me to take little steps and I learned that as I take a small step in spite of my fear, my fear loses its grip on me. When I came to understand that everyone takes chances, I was able to slowly allow myself to open up and engage in outside relationships, one by one.
Recognizing what can and can't be changed	I learned to rid my life of negative and toxic people and circumstances. I learned that I must work only to change myself and not others, to be true to myself and my recovery.
Taking blame	Understand not everything is my fault, something bulimics tend to believe or convince themselves is the case. I now work hard to separate things I must take responsibility for from things that are the responsibility of others.
Witching hours	Recognize the time when it's the most difficult to fight the addiction to binging and purging. With most bulimics, evenings are a challenge because at that time we are most vulnerable and emotionally fragile, creating a ripe environment for an episode. To overcome this, I use tools such as making plans during these hours and reassuring myself I can do it, this too shall pass.

WITH JOHN

What	How
Open and honest dialog	Know I can tell him the truth, I don't have to lie. "I am having a tough day," "I threw up today," etc. Help your spouse learn to listen, sometimes without speaking, to create a nonjudgmental atmosphere of trust. This calms the situation and allows the bulimic to release verbally rather than through binging and purging.
It's OK	Help your spouse know, regardless of the fact he's used to fixing things, he cannot "fix" bulimia, and that it's okay to just listen and support. This can be a very difficult concept and reality for a man.
Coping	Jointly learn what bulimia truly is and how to be a married couple coping with it. This is best done in couple's therapy.
Informing	Discuss and assist your spouse in understanding the fundamentals of bulimia. Have him read about the disease and learn from experts even if he won't take your word for it.
Helping	Work together to facilitate your spouse's understanding of exactly how he can help.
Recovering	Understand this is a journey and recovery is a long process. This can be frustrating and difficult for someone who is logical and a problem solver. Bulimia is not something that XYZ will cure permanently. We spent years discussing the reality of bulimia and the lifelong effects it has on its sufferers. To this day, John comes periodically with me to therapy just to keep abreast of this and me overall.
Healthy communicating	Learn how to communicate in healthy ways and not through bulimia. When I'd tell John I was struggling or having a hard time, he knew that meant I was expressing myself as best I could. With that he would then use some of the helpful tools mentioned above to help me. Oftentimes we would just talk, go for a walk, or take a drive to help me ride out my anxiety and bulimic urges. We practiced engaging in communication like this in therapy so I could set aside my fears of rejection, abandonment, and unworthiness and communicate like an adult.

WITH JOHN

What	How
Emotional intimacy	Through honest and open dialog in a safe environment such as a therapy session, sufferers learn to let their loved one fully see them, warts and all. Because my natural tendency was to be reserved, I had to practice this by taking baby steps. As I practiced this over and over and John learned of my fears, we were able to build a more intimate relationship. Each day we try to spend quality time together such as talking for thirty minutes in our bedroom when he arrives home from work, so that we both can be heard and become more emotionally intimate.
Validating feelings	Understand that both partners have their own unique set of emotions and that is okay. They are neither right nor wrong, but they are important to validate and recognize. Each party owns his or her feelings and must try not to redirect, discredit, or fix them.

GROUP

What	How
Tools for healthier eating	Eliminate distractions while eating, i.e., no TV, reading, phone calls; put utensils down after every bite and do not rush though a meal without tasting it.
Communication skills	We'd practice by taking turns speaking and allowing the speaker to fully articulate his or her thoughts. Only when the speaker and therapist finished could crosstalk occur. By practicing "active listening," we learned to fully hear what the other sufferer was relaying, enabling us to be better listeners and communicators.
Reaching out	By sharing challenges in group therapy, I was able to talk with others, share their pain, and work with the therapist in challenging myself to find ways to reduce my anxiety so I wouldn't turn to bulimia. I also learned I was not alone.
Trigger foods	I will always have certain trigger foods but that's okay, because I am lucky I now know this.

GROUP

What	*How*
Taking each moment as it comes	Live for the now, not yesterday, not tomorrow. For example, when a bulimic has an event to attend that includes eating, the more common way of dealing with the anticipated stress is to binge and purge daily prior to the event, which is not living for the moment. Practicing ways to get around anxiety such as deep breathing, repeating that today, this moment, is the only moment that matters, helps create a sense of detachment from the event and its associated anxiety. Just as an anorexic has difficulty in the presence of food, so does the bulimic. Talking, sharing, and listening to others and how they overcome the emotion of choosing and eating helps in alleviating the anxiety and subsequent dependence. A brilliant tool the therapist recommended was to phone ahead if going to a restaurant and request that they fax a menu. That enables a person to plan the meal in advance and alleviate anxiety and angst.
Listening to hunger	Is it hunger pangs, light-headedness, empty feelings? Or is the hunger associated with emotions, feeling lonely, bored, frustrated, confused, depressed? If it is the former, I ask what it is I want to eat so as not to deprive myself of true hunger and set the stage for a binge. If it is the latter, then I ask what it is I need, i.e., human interaction, self-comfort, rest, pampering, etc. I use the tools I have accumulated and wait thirty minutes.
Taking a time-out	If I feel vulnerable, I call a friend, get on the Internet, or distract myself.
Sharing your story	It feels great and others like hearing it.

The following helped me because they enabled me to take time out from my false relationship and dependence on food and allowed me to regroup and live in the present. When bulimics find means other than food to release emotion, deal with a current situation, etc., it eventually becomes easier not to binge. I found these alternatives to be pivotal in my recovery, especially outside of therapy.

OUTSIDE OF THERAPY: ALTERNATIVES TO BINGING

Journaling	Baths	Listening to music
Arts and crafts	Crying and releasing feelings in private	Taking a nap
Playing with pets	Practicing riding the wave of compulsion, white knuckling	Doing odd jobs around the home
Exercising	Buying something	Daydreaming
Art lessons such as painting and drawing	Outdoor work/gardening	Watch TV
Walking, driving	Reading book	Attending a recovery meeting such as OA, CODA, ALANON
Talking, in person and on the phone	Volunteering	

At the same time as I was working on myself, I felt compelled to reach out and help someone else in return. Basically I needed to do something besides concentrate on me. Before John and I were in our new home for two months, and as I began my intensive therapy, I embarked on a careful search to find some type of volunteer work I could do for someone else in need. I found exactly what I wanted.

Chapter 18

Through the Looking Glass

"Court Appointed Special Advocates, this is Mary speaking," the voice on the other end of phone said. I had phoned the Contra Costa CASA program to volunteer my time as a CASA. What this entailed was representing a special needs foster child in court. A special needs foster child is one who needs additional attention because he or she has been abandoned, abused, and/or neglected. The child has difficulties above and beyond that of a typical foster child. With this program, I would work to build a relationship with the child, write reports concerning progress in such areas as school, health, foster home, and overall well-being, with the child's safety first and foremost. From there I would represent the child in court, usually once a quarter, speak in front of the judge, the social workers, lawyers, etc., and give them a full status report.

After a three-month training course I was ready for the big day. I would review files and select a child whose personal CASA I would be. Nervous I might choose a child who didn't like me, I submitted my request anyway, hoping for the best.

It's common to select a child who is fairly young, usually between ages three and seven. After reading numerous files, I felt something inside telling me to select one particular child. At eleven, Amanda wasn't one of the younger ones. She had a most traumatic background, but I found something special and different about her as I read through her file. Something told me she was the one.

Finally the day arrived when I would meet Amanda face to face. I tapped on the front door with excitement and trepidation. Her foster mother, Peggy, answered. "Jocelyn, please come in. Have a seat in the dining room." Peggy excused herself and went to retrieve Amanda. She was simply beautiful. Her flawless brown skin radiated, her big brown eyes sparkled, and her petite, soft frame was that of a lovely young girl soon to be a teenager. I found her breathtaking. She sat next to me, too timid to look me in the face. As we sipped our beverages, we all managed to have a small chat. My intuition was right—I knew from that moment I was lucky to have found her.

Soon Amanda and I started seeing one another twice a week. On Tuesdays I'd pick her up from school and spend the rest of the afternoon with her, dropping her home in the late evening. We'd go to the library to do some school work and afterwards the fun would begin. She loved fast food, so she was always willing and eager to go to McDonald's, Burger King, or KFC. To ensure I did not risk the temptation of trigger foods, I would eat something prior to taking her to one of these places. That way, I could enjoy her company without feeling deprived, a toxic state for a bulimic. I would watch her eat, then we'd go to the movies, shopping, or do some type of activity she liked.

On Saturdays we'd spend the entire day together, going to amusement parks, shows, playing miniature golf, and visiting the zoo. I cherished the time I spent with her. We got to know each other well, and soon I was better able to understand her and her complexities. I learned how to carefully choose my reaction or response to her questions or behaviors. Often foster children are afraid to get too close to anyone and have a detachment disorder. They put up their guard and retreat inward when feeling as if too much care is being shown to them. Like many others, Amanda would often stare out the car window or go long periods of time without talking to me. I didn't care. I believed in her. More than that, I saw myself in her—a young girl desperate to be loved and liked by parents and peers. Like me, Amanda had a roof over her head, clothes to wear, and food to eat, but like me, her heart was lonely. She looked everywhere to fill the void she felt, thankfully not with food.

So many times I wanted to tell her I understood, but I knew she wasn't mature enough to comprehend and fully appreciate my input. I did my best to work beside her and counsel her with different explanations as to why this or that incident happened. I tried everything I could think of to help her emotionally, all in the hope she would see how much I loved her. I thought if she let just one person into her heart then maybe that would prove to be enough for her to make it through her tough times, something I wished someone had done for me while I was growing up. Unfortunately, I never accomplished that goal.

As time progressed and my fondness for Amanda grew, it became increasingly difficult to have only the CASA relationship with her. I needed more than a day or two of spending time with her. I genuinely loved her. I felt she wanted more too. "Jocelyn, please take me home with you. Can't I come over? I want to see your house. Please?"

I wasn't able to honor her request. One of the very stringent rules is never to let a CASA child into the private home of the CASA or share too much personal information. I fully understood and respected the primary focus was on the overall welfare of the child, not the fun and games aspect. But it became harder for me when time and again Amanda would ask to come over. Perhaps it was all too sad because I saw a little girl struggling to survive in a chaotic world. I wanted to help. I wanted to make things better for her, better than what I had. John knew the passion and love I had towards Amanda. I'd share stories, telling him of all the challenges she faced. Through me, he shared the same passion and love for her.

"Jocelyn, this is Sherry," Amanda's social worker said. "I wanted to call to let you know we are going to remove Amanda from her current foster home. Her foster mother isn't able to handle her any longer. I am not certain where we will place her. I know we've talked about your relationship with Amanda, and that you and John would take her in if it came to that. I'd like you to consider that now."

What? Amanda had nowhere to go? How terrible to know you weren't wanted. How awful to feel that somebody cared so little about you they'd just give you back to Social Services. It was no secret that many of the foster kids knew they were no more than a paycheck to their foster parents, a lodger in the spare room.

After hanging up with Sherry, I immediately spoke to John, "I can't let Amanda be tossed from foster home to foster home. She needs love, support, patience ... she needs help with her education, she needs so much. We can give that to her." After a long and thoughtful conversation, John and I agreed to try and adopt her. If we had her, there would be no more moving from one foster home to another. There would be no more under-equipped, rundown, inner-city schools to attend. There would be no more lack of genuine love, support, and patience any longer. We were determined to make this happen.

Having to tell my therapist, Sarah, that I wanted to bring Amanda into my life permanently would be a different story. Sarah, out of professionalism and honesty, had to tell me she thought it wasn't a good idea. Amanda had a lot of challenges and so too did I. Sarah had witnessed firsthand the emotional roller coaster I rode when it came to Amanda. I would share my ups and downs as it related to my relationship with her. She knew how much I wanted to help Amanda and knew my love was unconditional. But she knew I needed to take care of myself too.

Sarah told me I needed a lot more time before my bulimia and inner child was at peace. It had been only a little over a year since we had first started working together. I had made a lot of progress, but there were so many more feelings, experiences, and emotions buried deep inside me we had not yet uncovered.

Knowing this, I still couldn't separate the fact that Amanda had changed me. I couldn't walk away from her. I perceived that as acting like my parents. I loathed the thought I might be like them. I knew I was given a chance to change myself through therapy, John, and the love and support I received. I believed Amanda deserved the same chance. I had enough at my disposal to feel empowered and able to give her a better quality of life than what she currently had.

John and I connected with the Martinez Child Services Organization and began the long process of becoming adoptive parents. We spent the next several months having our lives and home analyzed for any possible red flags—we passed all scrutiny with flying colors—and attended adoption classes each Saturday.

Even though John and I were willing to risk everything to help Amanda, we received negative feedback within the social services community. The instructors weren't supportive of our willingness to help, love, and support her, especially because we were a white family trying to adopt an Ethiopian teen. "Jocelyn, she is already at the age where the onset of her real problems will begin," Latoya, the counselor, said. And because we lived in Danville, basically a white, upper-class area, they seemed to believe our community would do more harm to Amanda than good. Strangely enough, Amanda was well beyond the normal adoption cut-off age of five. Her chances of being adopted or living anywhere other than foster homes were negligible. Social services always strived for permanent residency, but that mattered little in this case. After a long and very emotional battle, John and I were approved to be certified adoptive parents for Amanda. She could now live with us forever, or so we thought.

In August 2002 Amanda was away for a week enjoying one of the many summer camps she regularly attended. Anxious and excited, John and I waited at the Oakland bus terminal where we would greet her and take her home with us for a week's trial. Since she had never seen our home or the room we decorated especially for her, we couldn't wait to see her expression as she opened her bedroom door. "It's like a princess' room" she said.

We were thrilled to see her eyes bulge and a big smile on her face. "This is your room," we told her. "All the things in here are for you."

As the days passed, Amanda seemed to retreat further and further inward. I had learned in class it is typical for foster children to recoil, that it's best to give them their space, so that's what I did. Still, it was troubling for me to see her wanting to sleep far more than she needed as well as not wanting to spend time with John and me. We did our best to help her out of this state. We went to the movies, shopped for clothes for her, went swimming at the local pool, and tried to have as good a time as we could, given the shortness of the stay. But now something didn't feel right. Amanda wasn't happy at all. I didn't expect her to be jumping through hoops telling us how wonderful this opportunity was going to be for her. But I didn't expect her to push me away, slam doors, drop things on the floor, or speak unkindly to me.

Still, in the end, I wasn't going to give up. After dropping Amanda back into the care of her current foster mother, my heart wanted to reach out and grab her and tell her everything would be okay, that I understood, and that together the three of us could make it better for her. I wanted to tell her we wouldn't let her down. She walked away without even saying goodbye.

"Hello, Jocelyn, this is Sherry. I've met with Amanda and we had a talk. She has decided she'd rather live with another foster mom than come and live with you and John. Amanda feels she would be more comfortable living this way."

I was completely taken by surprise. I had no idea how to absorb this news, so I simply said, "Thank you, Sherry. I am terribly saddened by this news. Should Amanda change her mind, John and I love her and our door is always open."

Weeks passed and we thought we would still have Amanda in our lives. We would talk with her and spend time with her. But we never heard a word from her. We had no idea where she was. The last we knew she was going to live with an elderly lady who had several children already under her care and who had no room for her but would squeeze her in somehow. We didn't hear from Sherry either. I couldn't take the lack of communication any longer and phoned her. She told me Amanda was placed in a different home and would be with some of her four siblings. I was somewhat relieved to hear she would not be alone in a small, cramped apartment but would be with her sisters. My heart sank, though, as Sherry said not to expect to have contact with Amanda, at least for a while.

By the end of 2002 John and I felt that we had experienced more trials and tribulations in the first two years of being married than what many couples experience in a lifetime. Now with my therapy in full swing, my ability to better understand my eating disorder, Amanda coming in and out of our lives, we were faced with yet another major challenge. John's company, the one where he'd been working for nearly eight years, was downsizing. John was taken aback when the announcement came out: *At the end of this fiscal year we will be formally acquired by another company. With that, there will be many layoffs. We will be relocating only a few people from corporate. We are sorry for this but it is in the best interest of the company.*

Hundreds of people were being laid off. With the economy in a downward spiral and the dot.com crash in full swing, it would be difficult to secure another position, especially in the couple of months between the announcement and the actual closure. Many people left with no other job. John decided not to fight for his job, which would have meant moving to New Hampshire, the new location, and working for the newly merged company. He felt it was time to move on and try something new.

Even if he had elected to move on it would have been a stressful time. We were facing a serious financial crisis. All the extra money we had, and some loans, had gone to finance my intensive four-day-a-week therapy sessions. We had no money left in the bank. No savings, which meant no emergency funds. Now we panicked. Immediately we searched for a job, John specific and targeted, me any job. The help wanted ads, monster.com, newspapers, anything I could find. I was qualified for only mid-level sales, not high-paying, base-salaried jobs, but I applied regardless. I was offered more or less the very undesirable ones, especially the retail ones—long hours, early mornings, late evenings, weekends, and low pay. But I was willing to do what I had to do. I was just about to sign on for an outside retail sales position, when John received great news. He was offered a position on the executive team for a company in Orange County. We were elated. It was an excellent opportunity for him and it was located in California, not some small town in another state. We were both ready to move away from the area I grew up in and leave the ghosts of the past behind.

Chapter 19

The Greatest Gift

We were very fortunate to quickly find what would become our new home. "A view to die for," said Kathy, our real estate agent. "When there's no fog, you can see all the way out to Catalina Island. And the city lights are spectacular. This is a very quiet neighborhood. It's not only very desirable, but located central to all the necessary shops, freeways, and entertainment venues."

By the fourth day after moving in, I had unpacked and organized everything in the house. Box after box, I carefully placed our belongings in their new places. Without understanding the full scope of my feelings, I just knew that this would prove to be a wonderful home for John and me.

Once settled in, I was eager to continue my journey towards making a full recovery. I had been in therapy more than two years, seeing one therapist after another four days a week and working diligently on my own. But despite all the work, I wasn't fully recovered. I had made a lot of progress, but I wasn't entirely free of my pains and bulimic addictions.

To fulfill my dreams of total recovery, I had to continue my journey of learning to be me, my true and authentic self. I knew, regardless of where I lived, the disease would follow. I made the commitment to continue seeking therapy as well as reaching out in the community in any way I possibly could. Giving without expecting anything in return always made me feel good.

I made only a few phone calls before I connected with a wonderful therapist. She, too, like the therapists I had in Northern California, welcomed me with loving and open arms. From that point, I was able to pick up where I left off and continue to unwrap my pained inner child and learn new ways to live my life. Carol worked with me to further teach me how to undo and let go of the past feelings and negative experiences that continued to haunt me and debilitate my thinking at times. Little by little, I made progress. And little by little I was learning to be me.

Again with the same sentiment I carried in the past, I felt compelled to reach out and help others who were less fortunate. I found another wonderful organization where I could volunteer my time to help the clients who seek their services. This organization provided interview clothing, computer classes, resume and cover-letter writing, and other services to women in transition and adverse financial situations—the homeless, abandoned, abused, those living in shelters, etc. The goal was to enable women to support themselves and their families while enhancing their self esteem through the programs and services. In addition, John and I decided to sponsor a child through an Outreach Program. The reward I received from these endeavors was tenfold compared to my software sales job. Reaching out to others helped me in my journey to recover from bulimia. Just like any selfless act, this gave me great pleasure because I knew I could make a difference in someone's life.

I had been told I'd never be able to have children but in September 2003, I became pregnant. Bulimia, like anorexia, causes irregular periods, making it extremely difficult to conceive. But, I'd heard Dr. Kilmer's words correctly. "Jocelyn, the blood tests confirm you are pregnant." I didn't know how to feel. Was I elated or worried because I wasn't fully recovered? It mattered little now ... I was pregnant.

In a state of shock, John and I sat on our couch talking for hours about having a child. In the end, we couldn't deny our true feelings. We were exceedingly happy and couldn't wait for the arrival of our little baby. Finding out I was pregnant after believing I would never have any children of my own was overwhelming. I was going to be a mom. But several days later, I began to feel incredible pain in my pelvic area. "John, something is wrong. I just know it. I don't feel right." Then the bleeding began, heavy bleeding. I knew in my heart I lost our baby. We sought medical attention immediately, and the nightmare was confirmed.

Crying in the doctor's office, I asked, "Was it me? Did I cause this? I am trying to recover from bulimia. I'm working so hard to get better."

The gynecologist, Dr. Richter, could see the pain I was in. He could see how desperate I was not only in trying to get better, but in wanting a baby, this baby. After spending a long time in his office, Dr. Richter recommended we not give up. He said there were plenty of women out there who shared the same struggle. Most of these women tend not to disclose their eating disorders to their doctors for the very same reason that was haunting me now. *What am I thinking? Am I crazy for wanting a baby? Am I insane to bring a child into my life when I'm not fully cured?*

Dr. Richter helped me tell myself that I was not just a recovering bulimic, but also a good and loving person. I was more than an eating disorder. I knew I could be a wonderful, responsible, and loving parent. "Jocelyn, since you are in therapy and have made such huge strides in your recovery path, I'd like to refer you to a fertility specialist, Dr. Pierce. She is a wonderful doctor with an exceptional pedigree. Don't back out. I know you can do this. You've come too far."

Four and a half months later, John and I sat in Dr. Pierce's blue and yellow waiting room. Many other couples waited to see her, all with the hope of having their own child. "John, will Dr. Pierce think I'm mad? Will she tell me to go away, that she can't or won't help me?" I was overcome with fear and nervous about telling yet another person, especially a fertility doctor, that I struggled with bulimia, that I was in therapy and had made great strides, but I wasn't yet fully recovered.

I was worried because what had become my most cherished dream, to have a baby, might be crushed in just a few short minutes. This was the biggest decision I had ever made in my life. I felt like my entire future would be unveiled in a little room in just a moment's time. "Jocelyn and John, please come in. Have a seat. I've carefully looked over your files. I'd like to go through them now with you and then talk about the next steps."

Uh, God, here it comes. "Everything looks okay. Even with your total colostomy, you still can absorb nutrients because it is actually the small intestines that do the absorbing, not the large. As far as your overall health, I don't see anything alarming. All your vitals are good and you seem in excellent condition. Now let's talk about the bulimia."

Sweat began to race down my spine. I looked to John for some reassurance. He smiled and patted my leg. My bottom lip began to quiver. Dr. Pierce continued, "I've had patients who weigh less than you and more than you. I see that you look healthy. I also understand you are in therapy. I am very pleased for that. I'd like you to continue your therapy. I will require that you do so. But because I can see that you have made great strides and have no real physical impairment that would cause me to caution moving forward, I'd like to run through the fertility process with you both. From there, we can take the next steps."

Did I hear right? Dr. Pierce didn't tell me I was insane, that there was no possible way I could have a baby. Did she say to me I was not just my bulimia, I was a person with other qualities too? I fell back into my chair. John turned and gave me another pat on my leg. This was going to happen. John and I were going to have a baby. I was going to be given the most precious gift in life, a child.

On February 28, 2004 I became pregnant. We conceived during our first month on Clomid. I couldn't believe it. We had beaten the odds—only twenty percent conceive during their first month. Within the first three months, we found out we were going to have a baby boy.

Chapter 20

Missing Pieces

One of the hardest and most painful parts of my recovery was the necessity for me to distance myself from my family, a situation that still endures. What the future holds I can't say but for now I need to remove influences that are toxic to me regardless of whether they are deliberate or perpetuated out of habit and ignorance.

Making the decision to isolate myself from my parents and sisters has not been an easy one or one taken lightly. I resisted it for a long time. As extreme as this may seem, I have communicated with many recovering bulimics and anorexics whose condition also required such radical measures. Many will eventually reconcile when they are strong enough to feel confident about who they are and to be impervious to whatever family dynamics once had such a devastating impact on them. A few, however, never reach that point and separate permanently to survive. Which I will be, I can't say with any level of confidence right now. Only time will tell.

My sisters and I had always had relationships punctuated with moments of real love and kindness but characterized in general by negativity. I take my share of responsibility for this and understand now from the vantage point of many years of therapy and introspection, that their behaviors were manifestations of their own wounds and hurt suffered during their formative years within the dysfunction that defined our family. They have their own journeys to take, and I hope one day they will be able to see me for me, and not the perceived, messed-up little sister who stumbled from one disaster to another.

My parents are now elderly and I'm sure are burdened today with many regrets about how things transpired. It is a timely reminder to me as I build my family that everyone gets only one shot at this and ignorance is not an excuse. I truly wish they had taken the time to try and understand what bulimia was back when I was seventeen or at any time in the intervening painful years. But they did not and so my commitment to my recovery means I must, for now, separate myself from the words and actions that ignorance permits.

I share these thoughts with you not because I believe every person with an eating disorder needs to separate from his or her parents and siblings. Far from it—I would not wish this extreme measure on anyone. But what I do want to stress is that a sufferer cannot recover alone. Parents, siblings, friends, lovers, spouses all need to grow and actively partake in the recovery. Ignorance is not an option in this information age where bookstores are filled with publications that can enlighten and inspire and the Internet is overflowing with resources, personal stories, and organizations that can help.

We must not be idle observers in the recovery process of someone we love or who is close to us. We owe it to our relationship to educate ourselves. In this way, I hope you as sufferer or loved one never has to endure the pain of enforced separation.

Chapter 21

A Husband's Story

That evening on the couch in our Northern California home when I finally confronted Jocelyn about her bulimia is as fresh to me today as when it happened. Not because of the shock of discovering the truth, but rather the realization of my own naiveté. In the nine months we lived together, I had blindly accepted her explanations of the extended and frequent visits to the bathroom. In addition, I had ignored or overlooked the fact we seemed to be forever shopping for groceries, despite not being big eaters. Above all, I had somehow dismissed her obsession with calorie counting and the fact that attempts to eat out always seemed to be tense occasions. Although I consider myself an intelligent and perceptive individual, I failed to see what was happening right in front of me. It was obvious that my new wife was in pain, both physical and emotional, but I simply figured by building a good, loving home and a rock-steady marriage, the pain would subside with time.

What I am trying to say is don't waste time in denial. If you think a significant other, family member, or friend is in the grips of bulimia, don't rationalize and talk yourself out of approaching the person. Just make sure you create the right environment for the sufferer to be able to be honest with you. Don't be judgmental or accusatory. Express your love, support, and help any way you can. Bulimics are crying out for help, they just don't know how to articulate it. If they feel threatened, they will retreat far into themselves. Approach with tenderness and love, and you have a far better chance of getting the desired response.

Another major consideration is that bulimics are incredibly talented liars as well as being possessed of great cunning and stealth. I took Jocelyn on vacation to Ireland, my homeland, before we were married and before I knew of her bulimia. We spent fifteen days in hotel rooms, barely apart for more than a few minutes any given day. Later she admitted to me that because she was so nervous meeting my family and friends for the first time, she had been horribly bulimic the whole trip. I was dumbfounded. How could she have binged and purged so much when she was rarely be out of my sight? To this day I still don't know. Bulimics don't like to share their secrets, as they tend to feel humiliated by the things they do and the lengths they will go to do them. If you don't approach a bulimic in the right way and provide a non-threatening environment for them to come clean, chances are they will tell you such convincing lies, you may well doubt your suspicions.

My major piece of advice, and probably the hardest one to adopt, is to quickly admit to yourself you don't have the first clue about what drives an eating disorder. Any preconceived notions or logic or rationale will only get in the way of your helping the sufferer. The first thing you need to do is clear your mind, get on the Internet, buy a book, or contact an expert or even do all three simultaneously. This will save you much heartache and frustration. If, like me, you are used to fixing things at work, you are a great problem solver, a motivator of people, or the greatest project manager of all time, your first inclination will be to approach your loved one's eating disorder in the same way. You will think "Okay, now I need to set goals for her, drive her to achieve them, and measure the results, etc., etc." and this is a recipe for disaster. Resist this temptation at all costs and go learn about the disease first. Realize that by trying to motivate or set goals, you are adding to the pressure, expectations of failure, and the overwhelming guilt at letting you down the sufferer already feels. Get informed and then take baby steps.

Make sure the sufferer gets professional help from someone who specializes in eating disorders. This may sound harsh, but if you don't, you'll be wasting your time and as with Jocelyn's experience, the wrong therapist can have a negative impact. Once the sufferer is in therapy, trust your chosen professional. Your loved one's recovery will be slow and will have many highs and lows. You will see progress and then regression. You have to steel yourself for the journey.

The most helpful and profound thing for me was the recommendation by Jocelyn's therapist that she and I go to joint sessions with another therapist, Ashley, who also specialized in eating disorders. Our weekly visits to her over a period of nearly two years did much to help me understand and provide real support for Jocelyn as she battled this horrible disease. Ashley was insightful and an expert at drawing out Jocelyn's feelings and fears and then translating them for me in a way I could understand.

I cannot stress the importance of joint sessions. I would recommend that anyone who is living with a sufferer find a therapist who does this, then participate together. Show the other person you want to learn and understand. Show you are there to give support and love. This, I guarantee you, is the quickest way to enable a sufferer to let you into her world to help. These sessions brought us much closer together and allowed us to feel we were battling a common enemy as a couple, painful as it was to watch Jocelyn pour out her anguish and cry so many tears that sometimes even Ashley looked like she might break down.

The final piece of advice I offer is to look after yourself. You need to make sure you do not become so consumed in your loved one's disease that you do not take care of your own emotional well-being. This disease will take a toll on you as you watch the triumphs and the failures, the steps forward and the steps back. You will feel anger at times, legitimate anger that requires an outlet. If you let the sufferer see how the whole situation is getting to you, though, he or she will feel guiltier. I will never forget Ashley telling me in one session that "Jocelyn already has enough guilt to fill up this whole room and now she is feeling guilty because she is not getting better quick enough for you."

Make sure you maintain interests outside of the battle for recovery. Once the sufferer is in good professional hands and you are well informed and are creating a loving environment, then make sure this disease does not become a 24/7 obsession for you. If it does, you run the risk of becoming frustrated and angry, and this will send the bulimic back underground.

I don't have all the answers, but I have learned a lot and made a lot of mistakes in the five years I have been privileged to spend with Jocelyn. I encourage you to never give up on your loved one, even if it looks like she has given up. Remember, more than anything else, the sufferer wants to be loved and accepted as she is. The best contribution you can make to recovery is to hold her and tell her you love her.

I have summed up ten recommendations for anyone who has a loved one suffering from bulimia:

1. If you have suspicions, you are probably correct. Approach the sufferer in a loving, non-threatening, open manner and create the environment for him or her to be honest.

2. Find a therapist who specializes in eating disorders and get your loved one an appointment as fast as you can.

3. Jettison anything you may think you know about eating disorders and set aside what you think is your natural talent for simply figuring things out.

4. Get on the Internet and/or down to the local bookshop immediately and read everything you can find on the particular disorder.*

5. See if the therapist will allow you to come to some of the sessions with the sufferer so that the therapist can educate you about how to help and, if not, then ask the therapist to recommend another one who you both can see.

6. Trust the professionals and if you are having doubts about the recovery progress, call the therapists for reassurance.

7. Allow yourself to be angry at the disease and at the circumstances or people who contributed to it, but find an outlet for this anger so it does not eat away inside you.

8. Make sure you keep up your interests or hobbies and don't allow the disease to take over your whole life. Your loved one needs your strength and support to recover. Allow yourself time off to recoup before heading back into the fray.

9. Find a simple way of communicating so you can gauge how well your loved one is doing without interrogating. We use, "Did you have a good day?" and if the answer is yes, then I tell her I am proud of her. If the answer is no, I simply say "It's okay, start again tomorrow."

10. Finally, when in doubt about what to say or do, default to expressing your love and then hold her. You will never go wrong with this and she will never get tired of the reassurance.

*Recommended books and Web sites:

- *Bulimia: A Guide to Recovery* by Lindsey Hall and Leigh Cohn
- *Handbook of Eating Disorders: Physiology, Psychology, and Treatment of Obesity, Anorexia, and Bulimia* by Kelly D. Brownell, John P. Foreyt (Editor)
- http://www.something-fishy.org/
- http://www.anred.com/
- http://www.mirror-mirror.org/eatdis.htm
- http://www.bulimia.com/
- http://www.edreferral.com/bulimia_nervosa.htm
- http://www.pale-reflections.com/bulimia.asp

My wife has battled this disease for twenty-three years, and we are finally seeing the light at the end of the tunnel after four years of intense therapy. You will, too, through hard work and dedication. Good luck and have faith.

Epilogue
The Beginning of the Beginning

The sum of my life's experiences, especially in my formative years, without question paved the path for my one-on-one battle with me as self and me as bulimic. Bulimia became my panacea to everything. Ironically, without it I might not be here today. It served its purpose, but now it's time for me to move on. Today I am no longer afraid. I do not live in my own world; rather, I live in the world everyone else lives in. I do not walk in the shadow with my head down. I see, feel, hear, and do things now as a thirty-five-year-old, not as a thirteen- or fifteen-year-old. I have finally grown up and am eager to see how my life will unfold.

I no longer allow the monstrous disease of bulimia to smother my fears, pains, and emotions, whether they are good, bad, or indifferent. I can look them directly in the eye, not turn my back, stuff them down, or have a bulimic episode. It's a constant daily battle, but I know now that I have the inner fortitude, along with the support from loved ones and others with eating disorders, to empower me to empower myself. I can let go, go along for the ride, and not worry if it's going too fast or too slow.

I no longer fear that the rest of my life will be filled with daily runs to the local McDonald's or nearest convenience store, only to rush home and stare at the cold white porcelain god I have come to know better than myself. I no longer fear I have to replace all the food in the refrigerator and cupboards before John gets home, hoping he doesn't notice the absurd amounts of money I waste on this unfulfilling quest for peace of mind. Most importantly, I no longer fear that my next bulimic episode may be my final dance with death. I use other things to fill my voids instead of food. I know what I never knew before, that I am me, someone more than my appearance. I have an inner depth and many attributes. Believing this, I can make healthy decisions instead of unhealthy ones.

I will forever be on a journey of learning just who I am. But what a wonderful journey it is. How free I feel now that so many doors have been opened and I finally see the other side. It's far prettier than bulimia's dark, enclosed caves. I don't think the real struggle between my bulimic self and my authentic self will ever fully be over, but I know it can be contained. I now take my bulimia to a quiet place. The more time I spend away from its debilitating and life-threatening grip, the more time I spend with my loved ones and being my true, authentic self. I am truly happy. I am learning to be me.

Now my life begins ...

If you would like to communicate with me or others who share the same type of experiences, please visit my Web site at: www.learningtobeme.com

About the Author

Jocelyn Golden, a native of California and a graduate of San Diego State University, has battled an extreme form of Bulimia for over twenty-three years. Golden wrote *Learning To Be Me* with the encouragement of some of her therapists who, despite having a combined total of over seventy years treating eating disorders, had never seen such an entrenched and extreme manifestation of the disease. Today Golden has her own Web site, www.learningtobeme.com, where she offers help and support to other sufferers and their families. Through her site she has not only helped people from all over the United States, but also all over the world, including Canada, China, Romania, Great Britain, and Australia to mention a few. An avid student of the disease, Golden has at the request of therapists met and spoken with the families of sufferers to help them better understand their loved ones' disease. Now resident in Washington DC Metro, Golden is committed to helping raise awareness about what she considers a silent but growing epidemic.

Jocelyn welcomes e-mails from sufferers and their friends and families and can be contacted directly at Jocelyn@learningtobeme.com

978-1-58348-482-1
1-58348-482-5

Made in the USA